Carey,
and Cultural
Transformation

Other titles by Vishal Mangalwadi

Missionary Conspiracy
Letters to a Postmodern Hindu
The World of Gurus
Truth and Social Reform
In Search of Self: Beyond The New Age

Carey, Christ and Cultural Transformation

The Life and Influence of William Carey

Ruth and Vishal Mangalwadi

**With Foreword by Tetsunao Yamamori
(President, Food for the Hungry International)**

**and Study Guide by Darrow Miller
(Vice-President, Staff Development,
Food For The Hungry International)**

OM
publishing

Copyright © 1993 Vishal and Ruth Mangalwadi

First published 1993 by Nivedit Good Books Distributors Private Ltd.
under the title *William Carey: A Tribute by an Indian Woman*

This Revised Edition published 1997 by OM Publishing

02 01 00 99 98 97   7 6 5 4 3 2 1

OM Publishing is an imprint of Paternoster Publishing,
P.O. Box 300, Carlisle, Cumbria, CA3 0QS, U.K.

Section headed *Study Guide* was prepared by Darrow L. Miller, Vice -
President for Staff Development, Food for the Hungry International
Copyright © 1997 Food for the Hungry, 7729 East Greenway Road,
Scottsdale, Arizona

British Library Cataloguing in Publication Data

A catalogue record for this book is available from the British Library

ISBN 1–85078–258–x

Typeset by WestKey Ltd., Falmouth
and printed in the UK by Mackays of Chatham PLC, Kent

Contents

**Dedicated to the missionaries
who loved the Indian Subcontinent enough
to serve with little recognition or gratitude.**

Acknowledgements

The First Chapter was presented by Vishal Mangalwadi, as part of a paper at Wetzlar (Germany), at the conference of the International Christian Media Commission, from 11-15 September 1988.

The Second and Fourth Chapters are revised versions of papers read by Ruth and Vishal respectively, at the William Carey Symposium, at the Presbyterian Theological Seminary, Dehra Dun, U.P., (India) in October 1991. The third chapter grew out of Ruth's lectures at the International Management Team's Conference of the Food For The Hungry International at Mombasa, in September, 1995.

The One Act Play was written and directed by Ruth for a worship service on August 4, 1991 at St. Paul's Church, Landour.

We are grateful to the organizers of the conference and the symposium, and to Carol Alter, the then Secretary of St. Paul's, for the opportunity and the encouragement.

For making this book possible , we are grateful:

to Mr. Sunil Chatterjee and Dr. &Mrs. J.T.K. Daniel of the Serampore College for their sacrificial assistance and hospitality during our visits to the William Carey Library;

to Roger and Jane Hedlund, Howard and Jill Wilkins and Prabhu and Philippa Guptara for their encourage-to Marietta Smith and Jenny Taylor for editing the mauscript;

to Ted West, Mrs. Ruth Unrau, and our older daughter Nivedit, for their assistance in proof-reading;

to the librarians of the Cambridge Brotherhood at Delhi, the Presbyterian Theological Seminary at Dehra Dun, the Woodstock School at Mussoorie, and the Bishop's College at Calcutta for the use of their resources;

to Albert and Audrey Amritanand and to Glenn and Marilyn Miller for their hospitality during our research trips to Calcutta;

and for this revised edition, we are grateful to Darrow Miller, Prabhu Guptara and David Porter for their inspiration, encouragement and support; to Darrow Miller, for preparing the Study-Guide, (initially for the FHI conference in Mombasa); and to Dr. Yamamori for his kind foreword.

Preface

Protestants do not confer sainthood on individuals, because the Bible calls everyone 'in Christ', a saint. However, if they did select 'special saints', William Carey would be a foremost candidate.

Carey arrived in India in 1793 as a missionary-reformer. This book is a tribute to celebrate the Bicentenary of his arrival. He deserves to be remembered; his contribution to India is unique. Yet most Indian historians have tended to ignore him. It is not Indian culture to say 'thank you'. Historians, however, are expected to be better. And we are grateful that the Government of India has honoured him by releasing a commemorative postage stamp.

One of Carey's biographers, George Smith, wrote that he was compiling his information in the hope that one day, a son of India would write on Carey. We are grateful that we – a son and daughter, for this book is a joint effort – can now fulfil that dream.

Our interest in Carey is not merely historical; we have lived and worked in the villages of India in the sphere of socio-economic development, and Vishal has also worked in the headquarters of two national political parties; these experiences have convinced us that neither currently popular 'development' programmes nor political action are adequate to meet India's basic needs. In order to intercept India's retreat into a new dark age we need to understand the essence of that (historically proven) process of modernization which William Carey started.

This book is not a biography. It aims to stimulate reflection and action. As such it is a sequel to Vishal's book *Truth And Social Reform*, and an example that illustrates the thesis of Francis Schaeffer's book, *A Christian Manifesto*.

Ruth and Vishal Mangalwadi
Mussoorie, March 1, 1993

Foreword

by Dr Tetsunao Yamamori, President of Food for the Hungry International

Carey, Christ and Cultural Transformation by Ruth and Vishal Mangalwadi is a welcome addition to the existing literature about the life and work of the missionary-reformer to India. The current volume brings out the multifaceted contributions Carey has made toward the modernization of India which the earlier publications have tended to ignore.

The India of Carey's days was marked by moral, social, intellectual and spiritual obscurantism. In the name of religion infants were sacrificed. Widow-burning was widely practised. Carey fought the custom of having girls married off young, by advocating female education. He championed the restoration of the innate dignity of women.

The book sketches Carey not only as a social reformer but as a missionary with clearly defined theological assumptions which undergirded all he did. In his mind, there was a correlation between conversion and reform and both were necessary ingredients for modernization. Our stubborn refusal to place ourselves under God's moral authority causes problems in ourselves as well as in our society. Without turning to God in absolute repentance (conversion) neither we nor our societies can be assured of salvation or transformation.

Ruth and Vishal were special guests at a recent conference for the senior staff of Food for the Hungry International. They gave the same inspiring and compelling messages drawn from the life and thought of William Carey as are presented here. Our conference, in large measure, dealt with the issues of effectively implementing holistic ministry. Ruth and Vishal were right on target with their presentations elucidating Carey's approach to individual and social ills: 'false beliefs lead to wrong behaviour and harmful culture.' In the end, the battle must be fought inside the mind of each person and Carey the missionary devoted himself to preaching, teaching and translating Scripture in order to fill the Indian mind with the truth of God's word.

Carey's integrated approach needs to be shared widely with those involved in Christian relief and development. Furthermore, Carey has a lot to say about the strategic response needed in today's mission context. The physically poor and those in need of the gospel live largely in the same geographical areas, concentrated in Asia, North Africa, and the Middle East. In fact, 82 per cent of the world's poorest, and almost 80 per cent of the world's non-Christians live here – places where traditional missionaries are not permitted. These areas are heavily under the influence of the world's largest gospel-resistant religions: Islam, Hinduism, and Buddhism. Only a fraction of the world's church resources go to these areas. In short, the materially poor are, at the same time, those in need of the Gospel. How then are we to respond?

Carey, Christ and Cultural Transformations provides rich insights by way of answer to such a question. While being hailed as the father of the modern missionary movement, Carey is little known for this strategic viability of the Great Commission today. I am glad Ruth and Vishal have taken time to bring out this volume for a wider audience.

1

A Quiz

Imagine a quiz master at the finals of the All India Universities' competition. He asks the best-informed Indian students, 'Who was William Carey?'

All hands go up simultaneously.

He decides to give everyone a chance to answer. The audience is asked to judge the correct answer.

'William Carey was the botanist,' answers a **Science student**, 'after whom *Careya herbacea* is named. It is one of the three varieties of Eucalyptus, found only in India.

'Carey brought the English daisy to India and introduced the Linnaean system to gardening. He also published the first books on science and natural history in India such as *Flora Indica*, because he believed the biblical view, 'All Thy Works praise Thee, O Lord.' Carey believed that nature is declared 'good' by its Creator; it is not *maya* (illusion), to be shunned, but a subject worthy of human study. He frequently lectured on science and tried to inject a basic scientific presupposition into the Indian mind that even lowly insects are not souls in bondage, but creatures worthy of our attention.

'William Carey was the first Englishman to introduce the steam engine to India, and the first to make indigenous paper for the publishing industry,' pipes up the student of **Mechanical Engineering**. 'Carey encouraged Indian blacksmiths to make copies of his engine using local materials and skills.'

'William Carey was a missionary,' announces an **Economics major**, 'who introduced the idea of Savings Banks to India, to fight the all-pervasive social evil of usury. Carey believed that God, being righteous, hated usury, and thought that lending at the interest of 36–72 per cent made investment, industry, commerce and the economic development of India impossible.'

'The moral dimensions of Carey's economic efforts,' the student continues, 'have assumed special importance in India, since the trustworthiness of the Savings Banks has become questionable, due to the greed and corruption of the bankers, and the nationalization of the banks, in the name of socialism. The all-pervasive culture of bribery has, in many cases, pushed the interest rates up to as much as 100 per cent, and made credit unavailable to honest entrepreneurs.'

'In order to attract European capital to India and to modernize Indian agriculture, economy, and industry, Carey also advocated the policy that Europeans should be allowed to own land and property in India. Initially the British Government was against such a policy because of its questionable results in the United States. But by the time of Carey's death, the same Government had acknowledged the far-reaching economic wisdom of his stand. Just as our Indian Government, after one-half century of destructive xenophobia, has again opened the doors for Western capital and industry.'

'William Carey was the first man,' asserts a **Medical student**, 'who led the campaign for a humane treatment for leprosy patients. Until his time they were sometimes buried or burned alive in India because of the belief that a violent end purified the body and ensured transmigration into a healthy new existence. Natural death by disease was believed to result in four successive births, and a fifth as a leper. Carey believed that Jesus' love touches leprosy patients so they should be cared for.'

The student of **Printing Technology** stands up next. 'Dr William Carey is the father of print technology in India. He brought to India the modern science of printing and publishing and then taught and developed it. He built what was then the largest press in India. Most printers had to buy their fonts from his Mission Press at Serampore.'

'William Carey,' responds a student of **Mass Communications,** 'was a Christian missionary who established the first newspaper ever printed in any oriental language because Carey believed that, "Above all forms of truth and faith, Christianity seeks free discussion". His English-language journal, *Friend of India,* was the force that gave birth to the Social Reform Movement in India in the first half of the nineteenth century.'

'William Carey was the founder of the Agri-Horticultural Society in the 1820s, thirty years before the Royal Agricultural Society was established in England', says the post-graduate student of **Agriculture**. 'Carey did a systematic survey of agriculture in India, wrote for agriculture reform in the journal, *Asiatic Researches*, and exposed the evils of the indigo cultivation system two generations before it collapsed.'

'Carey did all this,' adds the agriculturist, 'not because he was hired to do it, but because he was horrified to see that three-fifths of one of the finest countries in the world, full of industrious inhabitants, had been allowed to become an uncultivated jungle abandoned to wild beasts and serpents.'

'Carey was the first man to translate and publish great Indian religious classics such as the *Ramayana,* and philosophical treaties such as *Samkhya* into English,' says the student of **Literature**. 'Carey transformed Bengali, which was previously considered 'fit only for demons and women' into the foremost literary language of India. He wrote Gospel ballads in Bengali to bring the Hindu love of musical recitations to the service of his Lord. He also wrote the first Sanskrit dictionary for scholars.'

'Carey was a British cobbler,' joins in the student of **Education**, 'who became a professor of Bengali, Sanskrit and Marathi at the Fort William College in Calcutta where civil servants were trained. Carey began dozens of schools for Indian children of all castes and launched the first college in Asia at Serampore, near Calcutta. He wanted to develop the Indian mind and liberate it from the darkness of superstition. For nearly three thousand years, India's religious culture had denied to most Indians free access to knowledge, and the Hindu, Mughal, and British rulers had gone along with this high caste strategy of keeping the masses in the bondage of ignorance. Carey displayed enormous spiritual strength in standing against the priests, who had a vested interest in depriving the masses of the freedom and power that comes from knowledge of truth.'

'William Carey introduced the study of Astronomy into the Subcontinent,' declares a student of **Mathematics**. He cared deeply about the destructive cultural ramifications of astrology: fatalism, superstitious fear and an inability to organize and manage time.

'Carey wanted to introduce India to the scientific culture of astronomy. He did not believe that the heavenly bodies were "deities that governed our lives". He knew that human beings are created to govern nature, and that the sun, moon, and the planets are created to assist us in our task of governing. Carey thought that the heavenly bodies ought to be carefully studied since the Creator had made them to be signs or markers. They help divide the monotony of the universe of space into directions – East, West, North and South – and of time into days, years, and seasons. They make it possible for us to devise calendars; to study geography and history; to plan our lives, our work and our societies. The culture of astronomy sets us free to be rulers, whereas the culture of astrology makes us subjects, our lives determined by our stars.'

A post-graduate student of **Library Science** stands up next. 'William Carey', she reveals, 'pioneered the idea of lending libraries in the Subcontinent.

'While the East India Company was importing shiploads of ammunition and soldiers to subdue India, Carey asked his friends in the Baptist Missionary Society to load educational books and seeds into those same ships. He believed that would facilitate his task of regenerating Indian soil and empowering Indian people to embrace ideas that would generate freedom of mind. Carey's objective was to create indigenous literature in the vernacular. But until such indigenous literature was available, Indians needed to receive knowledge and wisdom from around the world to catch up quickly with other cultures. He wanted to make worldwide information available to Indians through lending libraries.'

'William Carey was an evangelist,' maintains the **student from the Indian Forest Institute.** 'He thought that "if the Gospel flourishes in India, the wilderness will, in every respect, become a fruitful field." He became the first man in India to write essays on forestry, almost fifty years before the government made its very first attempt at forest conservation, in Malabar. Carey both practiced and vigorously advocated the cultivation of timber, giving practical advice on how to plant trees for environmental, agricultural and commercial purposes. His motivation came from his belief that God has made man responsible for the earth. It was in response to Carey's journal, *Friend of India*, that the government first appointed Dr Brandis of Bonn to care for the forests of Burma and arranged for the supervision of the forests of South India by Dr Clegham.'

'William Carey', argues a feminist **Social Science scholar**, 'was the first man to stand against both the ruthless murders and the widespread oppression of women, virtually synonymous with Hinduism in the eighteenth and nineteenth centuries. The male in India was crushing the female through polygamy, female infanticide, child marriage, widow-burning, euthanasia and forced female illiteracy, all sanctioned by religion. The British Government timidly accepted these social evils as being an irreversible and intrinsic part of India's religious mores. Carey began to conduct systematic sociological and scriptural research. He published his reports in order to raise public opinion and protest both in Bengal and in England. He influenced a whole generation of civil servants, his students at Fort William College, to resist these evils. Carey opened schools for girls. When widows converted to Christianity, he arranged marriages for them. It was Carey's persistent battle against *sati* for twenty-five years which finally led to Lord Bentinck's famous Edict in 1829, banning one of the most abominable of all religious practices in the world: widow-burning.'

'William Carey was an English missionary,' pronounces a student of **Public Administration,** 'who initially was not allowed to enter British India because the East India Company was against proselytizing of Hindus. Therefore, Carey worked in the Danish territory of Serampore. But because the Company could not find a suitable professor of Bengali for Fort William College, he was later invited to teach there. During his professorship, lasting thirty years, Carey transformed the ethos of the British administration from indifferent imperial exploitation to "civil" service.'

'William Carey', reflects a student of **Indian Philosophy**, 'was a preacher who revived the ancient idea that ethics and morality were inseparable from religion. This had been an important assumption underlying the *Vedic* religion. But the *Upanishadic* teachers separated ethics from spirituality. They thought that the human self

(*Atman*) was the divine Self (*Brahma*). Therefore, our spirit cannot sin. Our *Atman* only gets deluded and begins to imagine itself as distinct from God. What we require is not deliverance from sin but enlightenment, i.e. a direct experience of our divinity. This denial of human sinfulness and emphasis on the mystical experience of our divinity made it possible for us in India to be intensely "religious", yet at the same time unabashedly immoral.

'Carey began to affirm that human beings were sinners and needed both forgiveness for sin and deliverance from its power over them. He taught that it was not ignorance but sin that had separated us from God; therefore, it was impossible to please God without holiness. According to him, true spirituality began only when we repented of our sin. This teaching revolutionized the nineteenth century religious scene in India. For example, after Raja Ram Mohun Roy, one of the greatest Hindu scholars of the nineteenth century, came in contact with Carey and the other missionaries at Serampore, he began to question seriously the spirituality then prevalent in India. He summed up his conclusions thus:

> The consequence of my long and uninterrupted researches into religious truth has been that I have found the doctrine of Christ more conducive to moral principles, and better adapted for the use of rational beings, than any other which has come to my knowledge.

A student of **History** stands up last. 'Dr William Carey is the father of the Indian Renaissance of the nineteenth and twentieth centuries. Hindu India had reached its intellectual, artistic, architectural, and literary zenith by the eleventh century AD. After the Absolute Monism of Adi Shankaracharya began to sweep the Indian sub-continent in the twelfth century, the creative springs of humanity dried up, and India's great decline began. The material environment, human rationality, and all that enriches human culture became suspect. Asceticism, untouchability, mysticism, the occult, superstition, idolatry, witchcraft, and oppressive beliefs and practices became the hallmark of Indian culture. The invasion, exploitation, and the resulting political dominance of foreign rulers made matters worse.

'Into this chaos Carey came and initiated the process of India's reform. He saw India not as a foreign country to be exploited, but as his heavenly Father's land to be loved and served, a society where truth, not ignorance, needed to rule. Carey's movement culminated in the birth of Indian nationalism and of India's subsequent independence. Carey believed that God's image was in man, not in idols; therefore, it was oppressed humanity that ought to be served. He believed in understanding and controlling nature instead of fearing, appeasing, or worshipping it; in developing one's intellect instead of killing it, as mysticism taught. He emphasized enjoying literature and culture instead of shunning it as *maya*. His this-worldly spirituality, with as strong an emphasis on justice and love for one's fellows, as on love for God, marked the turning-point of Indian culture from a downward to an upward trend. The early Indian leaders of the Hindu Renaissance, such as Raja Ram Mohun Roy, Keshub Chandra Sen and others, drew their inspiration from William Carey and the missionaries associated with him.'

So, who was William Carey?

Well, he was a pioneer of the modern missionary movement of the West, reaching out to all parts of the world; a pioneer of the Protestant Church in India; and the translator and/or publisher of the Bible in 40 different Indian languages. Carey was an evangelist who used every available medium to illumine every dark facet of Indian life with the light of truth. He is the central character in the story of the modernization of India.

2

William Carey – a Tribute by an Indian Woman

I love visiting Calcutta. Two hundred years after William Carey lived there, women are still treated more respectfully than in most parts of India.

In Lucknow in North India, where I grew up and went to a college, it was usual to be looked upon as a sex object. All my girlfriends accepted this fate. I too was unable to look upon myself as an individual with inherent dignity. It is liberating to be respected.

Calcutta was not always as courteous as it is now. Nor can we take it for granted that India will continue to treat women with civility. As she turns her back on the legacy of her reformers, her decline is predictable. The *Times of India*, (New Delhi, 22 May, 1993) reported the following about a university campus in North India:

> Parents are withdrawing their wards from the women's college as lumpen elements have been allowed access to the college premises, which includes girls' hostels, even at night – something unthinkable a couple of years ago. Most faculty members and students keep away from the University activities.

The result is that the once lively campus has been reduced to a fear-stricken place. The only solace for the administration is that the situation in most other universities in the country, particularly in Uttar Pradesh, is not any better.

Allahabad was an important matrix of literary and political influence before Independence, and gave us five Prime Ministers in the first four decades of freedom, including India's only woman Prime Minister – Indira Gandhi. Missionaries had transformed it into one of the premier educational centres in North India. Today, girls cannot walk freely on the campus.

The decline in respect for women in the institutes of learning ought to convince us that education by itself is not enough. It should also give us a glimpse of what a woman's life would have been had Carey not started his struggle. A brief review of his achievement in restoring women's God-given dignity and individuality will make it obvious why I choose to honour him.

The India that Carey saw

In his classic study, *Modern Religious Movements in India,* J.N. Farquar writes:

> When Carey came, Hindus were in a pitifully backward condition. Learning had almost ceased; ordinary education scarcely existed; spiritual religion was to be met only in the quietest places; and a coarse idolatry with cruel and immoral rites held all the great centers of population. Mohammedanism was very orthodox and ignorant, and steadily deteriorating. The collapse of their Governments and decline of the Muslim character had worked sad havoc in their religion. There was no living movement of thought, and no spiritual leader amongst them.

Needless to say women, being far behind men in most areas of culture and learning, were the saddest victims of this mental and spiritual deprivation. Sir W.W. Hunter observed in a similar vein:

> When Carey landed in India, Hinduism was in full vigour – its customs, traditions, institutions and laws all unchanged.

The country was practically untouched by any regenerative influence whatever. He had to encounter in its worst forms all the strength of the Hindu system.

'Where, O death, is thy sting?'

Carey's love for and dedication to the people of India is beyond dispute; yet he did not romanticize its darkness as so many of us do. The following excerpt from a letter written to John Williams in New York expresses his deep grief for India:

> No people can have more surrendered their reason. In business they are not deficient, but in religion they seem without understanding. But a people can hardly be better than their gods. They have made idols after their own hearts. Hindus have not the fierceness of American Indians, but this is abundantly made up for by cunning and deceit. Moral rectitude makes no part of their religious system; no wonder, therefore they are immersed in impurity.

Men may have surrendered their reason, but for women to attempt to develop or use it was sacrilegious. Superstitions and moral impurities are not abstract evils. Their practical consequence is to sear human conscience so effectively as to make life hell for the weak.

To another correspondent Carey wrote that no other land had seen such a lethal combination of 'false principles' as India. In other lands, he lamented:

> Conscience may often be appealed to with effect. Here God's law is erased thence, and idolatrous ceremony is engraved in its stead. The multitudes pay a thousand-fold more deference to the Brahmins than the people did to the priests in Papacy's darkest days. And all are bound to their present state by caste in breaking whose chains a man must endure to be renounced and abhorred by his wife, children and friends. Every tie that twines around the heart of a husband,

father and neighbour must be torn and broken, ere a man can give himself to Christ.

His journal often expresses the heaviness of Carey's heart. Here is a typical entry:

> Many [Hindus] say that the Gospel is the word of truth; but they abound so much in flattery and encomiums...that little can be said respecting their sincerity. The very common sins of lying and avarice are so universal also, that no European who has not witnessed it can form an idea of their various appearances: they will stoop to anything whatsoever to get a few cowries, and lie on every occasion.

'The sting of death is sin.'

'Sin enslaves', said Jesus. Many of us forget that slavery is a social reality. While slavery works to the advantage of some, it hurts the weak. In struggling for the emancipation of women, Carey was resisting the consequences of those sins that ruled India in his day.

Obviously women were not the only ones who suffered slavery. About the rigid caste system he writes:

> Perhaps this is one of the strongest chains with which the devil ever bound the children of men. This is my comfort, that God can break it.

Besides being oppressive, caste,

> ...cut off all motives to inquiry and exertion, and made stupid contentment the habit of their lives. Their minds resembled their mud homesteads, devoid of pictures, ornaments and books. Harmless, indifferent, vacant, they plod on in the path of their forefathers; and even truths in geography, astronomy, or any other science, if out of their beaten track, make no more impression on them than the sublimer truths of religion.

Carey, of course, did not note the above observation about

the distinctive condition of women. But women are primarily the homemakers. The absence of pictures and books in their mud homesteads was a reflection of the systematic emptying of the female mind – a mind which God had created to be filled with all that is intellectually true, morally noble, culturally good and aesthetically beautiful.

Yet, writes Carey's biographer S. Pearce Carey, he pitied more than blamed their superstition and servility, [which,] he would often say, came of long subservience, making him the keener to preach to these dull, passive captives. They had been so drilled to regard Brahmins as 'sort of half-divinities', that they attributed even the spots on the sun and moon and the sea's saltiness to their (Brahmins') vexed potent curses.

Kali, the goddess of death, is the patron deity of Calcutta and most other parts of Bengal where Carey came with the Good News of a God who died to give us life. Divinity was perceived in Bengal as *Ardhanareeshwara* – half male and half female – and yet women there were held in the lowest possible esteem. As a contemporary journalist Shakuntala Narasimhan puts it so aptly in her book on *sati*:

[Woman] was deified in the abstract and demeaned in real life...

It has been stated often enough that, 'In Hinduism there is no salvation for woman until she be reborn a man.' Her only hope lies in serving man in complete self-abnegation. Female infanticide, child marriage, *purdah*, dowry and *sati* were everyday realities accepted as normal by the learned pundits and illiterate masses. What was the common thread that linked all these practices together? Obviously an ignorance of the truth that woman shares with man the glory of being in God's own image; and the consequent diabolical trivialization of her God-given dignity. To quote, again, Shakuntala Narasimhan's description of the treatment of women:

Smothered or poisoned at birth, given away in marriage at a tender age, bargained over like some commodity by dowry-hungry in-laws, secluded in the name of chastity and religion, and finally burned for the exaltation of the family's honour, or shunned as inauspicious widow, the burden of oppression took different stages of a woman's life, from birth to death in a chain of attitudes linked by contempt for the female.

The Apostle Paul said that, 'The sting of death is sin.' The sins such as idolatry and caste resulted in death in more ways than one. Carey struggled against sin; he struggled to give the knowledge of truth about God; truth about who men and women really are as seen by their Creator, not as defined by the pundits; he struggled for freedom and for life.

Let us first examine some of Carey's struggles against various methods of murdering women, and then turn to his efforts for breaking the yoke of oppression.

'Where, O death, is thy victory?'

Infanticide

The widespread practice of exposing infants to death was then a 'religious' custom. It still exists today. If an infant was sick it was supposed that he was under the influence of an evil spirit. He was put into a basket and hung up for three days. Only if the child survived were means then used to save his life.

In 1794, near Malda, Carey had his first horrifying experience. He found the remains of an infant devoured by white ants after having been offered as a sacrifice. He could never be content after that with the mere telling of the story of a Saviour who had died for humanity, including the little ones. Carey felt obligated to struggle to save their lives.

Every winter at the Sagar *mela*, (where the sea and the

river Hooghly meet) children were pushed down the mud-banks into the sea either to drown or to be devoured by crocodiles, all in fulfilment of vows their mothers had made. This was looked upon as a most holy sacrifice; giving to Mother Ganges the fruit of their bodies for the sins of their souls.

As Carey's concern for these victims of superstitious beastliness became known, he was asked by the Governor General to inquire into the numbers, nature, and reasons for infanticide. Carey said that he took this assignment with great readiness. His report resulted in the practice being outlawed.

The moment of satisfaction came when Carey's group went to the Sagar *puja* (worship of the ocean), in 1804, to proclaim the story of God's own sacrifice. They found that due to administrative vigilance, not a single infant could be sacrificed to the goddess. What a victory: a wicked 'religious' practice had been suppressed.

Widowhood and widow-burning

When the much older husbands died, their widows were subjected to a terrible plight, because they were perceived as bad omens who had brought about the deaths of their husbands. It was believed that a widow had 'eaten her husband'. The widows, who were not victims of *sati*, had to live a life of austerity. This belief was a rationalization. The reality was that a widow was looked upon not as a precious individual in need of support to start a new life but as an economic liability. Her parents had already given the bride-price (dowry); the parents-in-law were not willing to part with their 'possessions' and return the dowry to get the young widow remarried. And, of course, the illiterate widow was in no position to earn and become an economic asset for the family.

To add insult to injury, the bereaved widow had to shave off her hair, remove all jewellery, and wear white, all to avoid attracting the other men in the family and causing them to go astray.

She had to be kept indoors to keep her chaste. Widows were generally not allowed to remarry, but *niyoga* (which is not the same as remarriage) was practiced. It meant that the widow was required to cohabit with her brother-in-law, or another male relative, for the purpose of producing a son to offer religious oblations for the deceased husband, if he had no sons of his own to undertake this important religious rite.

The Widow Remarriage Act did not come into effect until 1856, for the first time making it legal for a widow to remarry. Until then the only options for a widow were either to commit *sati* or to suffer life-long indignity and hardship. *Sati* often seemed the lesser of the two evils; therefore, the widows preferred a speedy death to the unknown horrors of future destiny. They were deluded into thinking that by their act of self-sacrifice they would bestow a celebrity status on the family, and would take seven generations of their family, before and after them, to heaven. They were assured that the heroic act of self-immolation would deify them as *sati-mata* and supremely, they would be considered *pativrata*.

Shuddhitatva describes a *pativrata* woman:

> All the actions of a woman should be the same as that of her husband. If her husband is happy, she should be happy, if he is sad, she should be sad, and if he is dead she should also die. Such a wife is called *pativrata*.

One evening at Naoserai in 1799, Carey witnessed the cruelty of *sati*. He gave the following moving description in a letter to Andrew Fuller:

> We saw a number of people assembled by the riverside. I asked for what they were met, and they told me, to burn the body of the dead man. I inquired if his wife would die with him; they answered, 'yes', and pointed to her.

She was standing by the pile of large billets of wood, on the top of which lay her husband's dead body. Her nearest relative stood by her; and near her was a basket of sweetmeats. I asked if this was her choice, or if she were brought to it by any improper influence. They answered that it was perfectly voluntary. I talked till reasoning was of no use, and then began to exclaim with all my might against what they were doing, telling them it was shocking murder. They told me it was a great act of holiness, and added in a very surly manner, that if I did not like to see it, I might go further off and desired me to do so. I said that I would not go, that I was determined to stay and see the murder, against which I should certainly bear witness at the tribunal of God.

I exhorted the widow not to throw away her life; to fear nothing, for no evil would follow her refusal to be burned. But in the most calm manner she mounted the pile, and danced on it with her hands extended, as if in the utmost tranquillity of spirit. Previous to this, the relative, whose office it was to set fire to the pile, led her five times round it – thrice at a time.

As she went round, she scattered the sweetmeats amongst the people, who ate them as a very holy thing. This being ended, she lay down beside the corpse, and put one arm under its neck, and the other over it, when a quantity of dry cocoa leaves and other substances were heaped over them to a considerable height, and then ghee was poured on the top. Two bamboos were then put over them, and held fast down, and fire put to the pile, which immediately blazed fiercely, owing to the dry and combustible materials of which it was composed.

No sooner was the fire kindled than all the people set up a great shout of joy; invoking Siva. It was impossible to have heard the woman, had she groaned, or even cried aloud, on account of the shoutings of the people, and again it was impossible for her to stir or struggle, by reason of the bamboos held down on her, like the levers of a press.

We made such objection to their use of these, insisting that it was undue force, to prevent her getting up when the fire burned. But they declared it was only to keep the fire from falling down. We could not bear to see more, and left them, exclaiming loudly against the murder, and filled with horror at what we had seen.

That funeral pyre set Carey's spirit aflame with anguish. His brain burned with her body. His sensitivity and compassion naturally extended over to the children who had lost their father. In their mother they would have had, at least, a natural guardian; their tenderest and most faithful and watchful friend. But her cruel death left them orphaned in one, sad day.

The culture which glorified this cruelty had clearly put family possessions above the intrinsic value of a woman's life. Carey vowed, (as did Abraham Lincoln in America later concerning the auction of slave women) '...to hit this accursed thing hard, if God should spare him'.

The weavers (*Kories*) buried their dead. So their widows had to be buried alive. Carey describes how a pit was dug and the widow sat in it with the body of her dead husband in her lap. The family then threw in mud,

> ...and after a short space, two of them descend into the grave and tread the earth firmly around the body of the widow. She sees the earth rising higher and higher around her without upbraiding her murderers, or making the least effort to arise and make her escape. At length the earth reaches the head of the suffocating widow – the mother.

The abolition of *sati*

In 1802 Lord Wellesley asked William Carey to institute an enquiry into *sati*. Carey sent out people who investigated carefully the cases of *sati* in a thirty-mile radius of Calcutta and they discovered the 'damning' total of 438 widow-burnings, '...the toll of a single year's superstition, cruelty and waste'.

Armed with these facts Carey implored the Government to ban *sati*. Tragically for the Indian widows, Lord

Wellesley had to leave India before he could take action, and his successors were unwilling to interfere with the religious sentiments of the people. The legal prohibition of *sati* was stalled for yet another quarter of a century.

Carey knew that Hindu polytheism is false in teaching that the husband is *'patidev'* - a woman's god. Marriage does not exhaust the totality of what a woman is. Therefore, Carey fought against the idea that a woman's life ceases to be valuable after her husband's death. We can be grateful that he did not see himself merely as a servant, but also as a fighter. Service, without fighting, can often mean only the strengthening of the social *status quo*.

For Carey 'fighting' did not merely mean 'agitating' as it so often means today. It also meant educating. Carey researched; and wrote. It was his article in his newspaper, *Friend of India*, which became the central document for debate on *sati*, in and outside the British Parliament.

Carey considered this battle against a social evil as a spiritual battle against religious darkness and the forces of death. He prayed and got others to pray. One of his prominent prayer partners in this matter was William Wilberforce, the Evangelical Member of Parliament in England and the leader of the movement for the abolition of Britain's slave trade. Wilberforce struggled in prayer for both the emancipation of the African slaves and for the plight of Indian women.

Carey's great day came when, on December 4, 1829, Lord Cavendish Bentinck, after one year of careful study, declared *sati* both illegal and criminal, by Regulation XVII of the Bengal Code. The edict was sent to Carey for translation on Sunday, December 6. Carey jumped with joy, abandoned his plan to preach on that Sunday, in order to carry out the 'fast unto the Lord', spoken of in Isaiah 58:6 and Proverbs 24:11. At long last widows were legally free to live as human beings, and no longer would children be cruelly orphaned in the name of 'religion'.

Breaking the yokes of oppression

Child marriage

Initially a sexually promiscuous society sounds free, but eventually it curtails a woman's liberty in order to protect her. The advocates of compulsory education have discovered that the parents will not send their daughter to a school if it means sending her as far as the next village. It is dangerous, since neither the men nor the girls themselves can be trusted. To guard her safety, and to uphold her family's honour, getting her married off at the earliest is the best safeguard. Childhood is thus denied to a girl. She has to pass into motherhood before she has time to grow as a person.

The last census of the nineteenth century in Bengal revealed that in and around Calcutta alone, there were ten thousand widows under the age of four, and over fifty thousand between the ages of five and nine. All these child widows were victims of child marriage.

Polygamy was also a common practice. Sometimes 50 women were given to one Brahmin man so that the family could boast that it was allied by marriage to a *Kulin* (high caste). Even Ram Mohun Roy, who later supported many of Carey's reforms, was married three times by his father when he was a child. His first wife died at a very early age. Then, when he was about nine years old, his father married him to two different wives within an interval of less than twelve months.

Child marriage was outlawed only in 1929 when the Child Marriages Restraint Act was introduced. However, this, as we all know, is only 'legislation on paper'. Even Cabinet ministers in some Indian states get their children married off at a tender age. No social problem, if it is rooted in the moral/religious soil of a culture, can be easily eradicated legally. Carey understood this, and did not agitate against child marriage as such. Instead, he sought to undercut its immoral roots through the teaching of the Bible, and its social roots through female education.

But the practice of child marriage tended to preclude the possibility of educating Indian women. This, in turn, deprived them of intellectual and cultural development. They became dependent and vulnerable to oppression, exploitation, and enslavement. In seeking to educate girls, Carey was also undermining their dependency, a chief source of their slavery.

Female education

The following statement of a Hindu father to a missionary about the education of his children is a typical example of the traditional Indian attitude which Carey had to confront:

> You may educate my sons, and open to them all the stores of knowledge: but my daughters you must not approach, however benevolent your designs. Their ignorance and seclusion are essentially necessary to the honour of my family; a consideration of far greater moment with me than any mental cultivation of which I cannot estimate the benefit. They must be married at an age when your plans of education could scarcely commence.

Hannah Marshman took on the educational problem. She was a decided asset to Carey's community in Serampore. A warm, pious and prudent woman, she not only ran the household, but she also started a boarding school for the children of missionaries and other Europeans. This was an exemplary contrast to what Indian housewives were allowed to do with their lives and talents. This venture also greatly helped defray the expenses of the Mission. By the end of the first year, in 1801, the boarding school showed a profit of Rs.300. With this success Mrs Marshman was able to start schools for Indian boys and girls.

The success resulted in the establishment of the Calcutta Baptist Female School Society in 1819, and an additional school for girls in Calcutta. During 1820–30, Carey's Mission in Serampore took the lead in bringing about the beginning of the revolution of modern education for the women of rural Bengal. And it sparked the founding of other girls' schools in Benares, Dacca, and Allahabad.

The immediate impact these schools began to make was apparent to all observers. Mrs Ann Judson, for example, wrote in a letter to her sister about the Mission Charity School near Dr. Carey's house,

> with two-hundred boys and nearly as many girls – chiefly children picked up from the streets, of no caste. We could see them kneel in prayer together, and hear them sing. It was most affecting.

Free schools for the low castes and the outcasts were always a chief feature of Carey's work, and these were started within a twenty-mile radius of Serampore where almost 8,000 children attended.

Carey did not limit himself to giving only a primary education to women. The Serampore College was launched in order to offer higher education in the vernacular. In 1827 Hannah's husband, Dr Marshman, obtained for Serampore a charter to confer degrees in all faculties, making it the first college in India to do so. Until today, the Serampore Senate remains the only University in India to confer degrees in Divinity.

These women missionaries pioneered education for women in India. Without their heroic and sacrificial efforts the feminine potential in India would still be untapped.

I got a feel for the price these women paid, when I came back to India from the USA, married Vishal, and in 1976, driven by my God-given love for India, went to live in rural Madhya Pradesh for the first eight years of my married life. The toilet was outdoors; drinking water had to come from three kilometers away; the nearest medical facilities were 13km away; and if we wanted to buy bread and butter, we had to travel over 200 km to Jhansi – a tortuous six-hour journey during and after the monsoons!

Both our daughters were born there. Rural life is not 'romantic' when you have to spend much of your energy in protecting your children, not merely from flies and mosquitoes, but also from snakes and scorpions falling from your thatched roof. I found it a daunting challenge to expose my daughters to the dangers of contagious diseases such as TB and leprosy in order to serve women who are not always cooperative, let alone understand me.

What would you do when a fifteen-year-old girl, whom you have struggled to help intellectually and culturally, is made pregnant by her step-father, and is quickly married off to prevent his sin from being exposed? Incidents such as these drove me to a sense of hopelessness: will my sacrifice, hard work and investment in a precious person amount to anything worthwhile in a climate as decadent as this? The blame cannot be put entirely on men. As I made many friends among the rural women I began to admire them. One of their strengths is their stubbornness. It allows them to smile through life in spite of their social deprivation, domestic oppression and natural hardships – crop failures, famines and floods. But stubbornness also means resistance to change even when they know it to be to their advantage. Stubbornness is the true custodian of the 'traditional' India.

Living and serving in rural India for years eventually drove William Carey's wife, Dorothy, insane – and I am not surprised. She was dramatically different from Hannah Marshman and her husband, William Carey. She had not initially consented to accompany her husband to India, but she was talked into changing her mind by

Carey's friend, the doctor John Thomas, and had to board the ship within twenty-four hours – too short a time to pack, let alone prepare herself for the hardships ahead. The ramifications of staying behind with four little children had been an alarming alternative.

Devastating circumstances overwhelmed Dorothy from the outset. She didn't share her husband's vision. And his many accomplishments in missions, linguistics, printing, journalism and social reform overshadowed her own struggles with poverty, child-rearing, the heat, mosquitoes, her bouts of chronic dysentery and the frequent upheavals as they moved house. All that William Carey was able to accomplish was possible only if he could leave the domestic responsibilities to his wife. But she paid a high price.

For Dorothy's sake, I would have been glad had Carey returned to England. For India's sake, I am grateful that he did not. For the Indian religious culture at that time was completely incapable of producing such a sacrificial missionary spirit.

Even now Hindu orthodoxy gives the impression of being much better at producing militant murderers – those who would revive *sati* if they could – than at motivating missionaries who could improve the condition of oppressed women.

Women, particularly in rural India, need not only state-sponsored development projects but also women missionaries such as Hannah Marshman. But our cultural insensitivity has resulted in a policy that refuses visas to missionaries who could improve the status of women. One of the most inhuman results of this policy is in the area of nursing care for the poor. The affluent in India can buy quality care. The poor have to accept constant humiliation in most of our hospitals. Indian culture, even today, does not honour those who serve. Most women who join the nursing profession do so out of economic necessity, not because of a sense of calling. Their cultural conditioning makes them see service as a humiliation and not a high privilege and they resent their profession and treat their patients harshly as a result.

Foundations for true freedom

The plight of the Indian woman (or, for that matter, the predicament of an untouchable man) was rooted in a lack of understanding of what a human being is – whether male or female. Secular education, by itself, cannot offer a high view of human life, any more than can Hinduism for, to the Indian mindset formed by notions of reincarnation, it makes us no more valuable than animals.

Raja Ram Mohun Roy, Carey's younger contemporary who reinforced many of Carey's reforms, put his finger on the basic problem when he said:

> The root of the whole wretched state of the Hindu society was idolatry and the obnoxious superstitions necessarily attached to it.

The later chapters in this book discuss how idolatry lowers a human being's dignity and darkens the mind. Carey lamented about India:

> Many perish with cold, many for lack of bread, and millions for lack of knowledge.

He knew that, as his dear window-plants were 'meant for the sunlight', so was woman-kind made for God. Women could not grow into a true knowledge of themselves, nor enter true liberty which enabled wholesome family and social life, unless they grew in their knowledge of him. Carey strove to make the knowledge of the Saviour available to Indian people.

When he was still on the ship to India, Carey overheard

some fishermen tell his companion, Thomas, that they were poor and, therefore, had not read the *Shastras* (the scriptures). Only those who were rich, they said, could read. This implied that spiritual enlightenment and education were reserved for those who had earned enough merit in a previous birth to be born rich or high caste or both. Women, for instance, needed to serve their men well in order to be reborn, hopefully, as men, and to be able, then, to search for salvation. It was partly this fisherman's insight which confirmed in Carey's mind the urgent need to translate, publish, and distribute the Bible, to make the Good News of salvation available to the poor and downtrodden – including the women of India.

This former shoemaker, William Carey, who was no academic, received the gift of 'tongues' from the Holy Spirit, to proclaim the Good News to many nationalities. With goal-oriented plodding, he learned many languages. With the help of many pundits he translated the Bible from the original Hebrew and Greek. He had no dictionaries or grammars to aid him. It was his Bible that informed us that women share with men the glory of being created in God's own image.

The results of making the Bible available were long-term – a true foundation for the work of transformation and salvation. In due time the teaching of the Bible undercut the (ir)religious foundations of infanticide, child marriage, *sati*, the burning and the burying of lepers and the sacrifice of human beings. By providing the theological foundations for a belief in the sacredness of human life – both male and female – and by demonstrating that the emancipation of India's women was possible, Carey made certain that his efforts would bless future generations as well as his own.

Indian Christian women

Carey knew that Indian women required their own 'kind': woman to woman. Only they could take the knowledge of the truth to the women in purdah. What a joy it must have been for William Carey when Jaymani became the first Bengali woman to be baptized, in January 1801. The reforming power of the Gospel could now flow to the coming generations with their mother's milk. Even Carey could not have foreseen that Jaymani's conversion was like the small cloud – 'as small as a man's hand' – which Elijah saw after three years of famine in Israel. That cloud was to cover the whole land and pour down showers of God's blessings. Within a century of Jaymani's conversion, Indian Christian women were to cover the Indian Subcontinent. And mass education and universal nursing care followed in its wake. The following observation about the role of Indian Christian women (quoted by J.N. Farquhar in his classic, *The Crown Of Hinduism*) was made by a Hindu in 1903:

> Though cut off from the parent community by religion and by prejudice and intolerance, the Indian Christian woman has been the evangelist of education to hundreds and thousands of Hindu homes. Simple, neat, and kindly, she has won her way to the recesses of orthodoxy, overcoming a strength and bitterness of prejudice of which few outsiders can have an adequate conception. As these sentences are being written, there rises before the mind's eye the picture of scores of tidy, gentle girls, trudging hot and dusty streets barefooted, under a scorching sun, to carry the light of knowledge to homes where they will not be admitted beyond the ante-chamber, and where they cannot get a glass of water without humiliation, yet never complaining, ever patient. To these brave and devoted women wherever they are, friends of female education all over the country will heartily wish 'God-speed'.

One hundred years ago, nursing care in India was almost

impossible to obtain, except through Indian Christian women. As we now celebrate the Bicentenary of Carey's arrival, that blessing of nursing care has overflowed across the seas to the Muslim nations of the Middle East where nursing care was unknown. Tens of thousands of Indian Christian nurses are serving the sick in the Gulf States. Often they are humiliated and sexually harassed by a people who think that these women are willing to serve men (who are not their husbands) because they are sexually permissive. The fact is that it is the permissiveness of our traditional cultures that had enslaved women.

The Gulf States, as well as India today, can buy services such as education and nursing care, but these societies have yet to realize fully that hygiene, cleanliness, efficiency, honesty and the overall output of a country is substantially dependent on the position given to women in that society. The irony is that today too many people in the West also need reminding that the salvation of women depends on conversion and moral transformation, not on worship of goddesses. Mr Surendranath Bannerjea, a noted nationalist and the editor of the *Bengalee* wrote the following, in 1911:

> We have worshipped the goddess of *Sakti* (i.e. energy) for centuries; how is it that through those very centuries we have remained so weak and helpless as a nation? We are the devout worshippers of *Sarasvat* (the goddess of learning); and at the same time have received a scant share of her blessings. The priests who are the monopolists of the religious rites and ministrations are for the most part as innocent of *Vedic* knowledge at the present day as the *Sudra* (the Untouchable) was in the days when the gates of knowledge were shut against him by the iron rules of caste. We offer our devotions to *Lakshmi* (the goddess of wealth) every recurrent year; and we remain none the less a nation of paupers.
>
> The orthodox Hindu makes a fetish of certain rules of hygiene formulated by his ancestors in the dim past; he regards it as

sin, for instance, to take his meals without bathing; or to remain in unwashed clothes for more than a day; but, with all his religious devotion to the traditional rules of cleanliness, he betrays a strange indifference to the principles of sanitation evolved by modern science, though plague and cholera and all the other diseases that are generated by filth are decimating thousands of his fellow men year after year...

The Hindu father blesses his son's wife with the invocation, 'May she be like *Sabitri'*. But was there room in ancient Hindu life for the Philistinism which actuates the modern Hindu father to huckster and chaffer over the price of his son with the unfortunate person in search of a bridegroom for his daughter?

It is tragic that a basic lesson that had been learned one hundred years ago by enlightened Indians, is now being forgotten. That lesson is that the hygiene, health and wealth of a nation is determined by the position given to women – and not by projects sanctioned by the World Bank, Unesco or the World Health Organization (WHO). The status of women is directly proportional to the level of moral purity in a society. And that is what conversion is all about. No wonder Carey was excited by Jaymani's conversion.

Conclusion: a suffering servant

William Carey's service was neither smooth nor easy. Struggle marked his life from beginning to end. The difficulties ranged from having a lack of food and funds to the suffering in his own family, and opposition – even from his own Mission Board in England. His group at Serampore often had to earn their own livelihood as well as funds for their projects. These difficulties would have discouraged anyone who seeks to serve in his own strength. This cobbler, who would have been an Untouchable if he had been born in India, plodded on with a goal and a purpose. The fact that he knew that God had commissioned him was one secret of his missionary dynamism. The other source of his sustaining vision was the knowledge that the Gospel was the only power that could liberate India. The Lord who sacrificed his own life to save sinners was both the inspiration and the supreme source of Carey's strength.

3

William Carey – a Jar of Clay

Was Carey a superman? A model beyond our reach? Not at all. He, like St. Paul, was conscious that 'we have this treasure in jars of clay'. The famous passage from 2 Corinthians 4:1–17 was very much the story of Carey's life: 'We are hard pressed on every side, but not crushed; perplexed, but not in despair; persecuted, but not abandoned; struck down, but not destroyed . . . For our light and momentary troubles are achieving for us an eternal glory that far outweighs them all.'

If you light a lamp and put it into a jar of clay you notice that it is through the cracks that the light shines. The solid parts of the jar prevent the light from radiating. It is often the 'cracked pots' that God chooses to use. William Carey was one such.

Can a woman write a tribute to William Carey after the way he treated his first wife? Dorothy's tragedy is indeed the darkest spot on Carey's life. He was human too.

Dorothy Carey's sacrifice

Dorothy Plackett Carey was twenty-five and William almost twenty when they married. She resisted going to India – in hindsight with good reason – but went nonetheless. Once there, with seven small children, and recurrent bouts of illness, she suffered immensely, as she had suspected – and eventually went insane.

Dorothy Carey unknowingly made a great sacrifice for the Gospel. Her illness was seen as a blot and an embarrassment on Carey's career. Even today mental illness is not something you talk about – even though it is still common in mission.

Biographers have dismissed Dorothy – William Carey's first wife of 26 years – in a few sentences. George Smith in his biography *The Life Of William Carey* writes:

> She never learned to share his aspirations or to understand his ideals. Not only did she remain to the last a peasant woman, with a reproachful tongue, but the early hardships of Calcutta and a fever and dysentery clouded the last twelve years of her life with madness.
>
> Almost from the first day of his early married life he had never known the delight of daily converse with a wife able to enter into his scholarly pursuits, and ever to stimulate him in his heavenly quest.

Another writer called her a 'dull commonplace woman' who was 'deplorably unsuited to be William's wife.'

Charlotte Yonge also said of her that 'she was a dull, ignorant woman, with no feeling for her husband's high aims or superior powers.' These are cruel words. James Beck writes in his book *Dorothy Carey:*

> Meanwhile many of these same authors have subjected William to a similar but opposite disservice: overpraise. Sometimes we cannot tell which does us more harm: harsh criticism or bloated praise.

There are also sweeping statements made by John Marshman who said:

> The extreme consideration and tenderness which invariably marked his conduct towards her, place the meekness and magnanimity of his character in the strongest light. No word of complaint escaped him.

But Carey did complain. In his journal he writes at the beginning of Dorothy's emotional retreat from reality, 'I don't love to be always complaining. Yet I always complain.' So to suggest that Dorothy's problems never bothered Carey, that he never uttered a word of complaint, or that he never lost patience with her is to place him in an untenable position. He was as human as she. We can, as Beck says, honour and remember him well without having to make ourselves believe he was perfect in all that he ever said or did.

It is true that instead of signing her register at her wedding, she put a sign – because she did not know how to read or write. This was not due to lack of intelligence; there simply was no village school where she grew up. She did later learn to read and write.

They were married for twelve years before William heard the call of God to be a missionary. They had already had six of their seven children when Carey set his heart on his mission – a very risky venture at that time. Dorothy had been adamant about not going with him. No amount of arguments or reasoning seemed to change her mind. Possibly intuition told her that 'it would be a sentence of banishment for her and the children', without being able to articulate her reason. Carey's own father had thought him 'mad' to go. Some of the factors she must have considered were that she was six months pregnant, already had three little sons, she probably had just gotten over her nausea and the thought of still more nausea – five months of sea-sickness – would have been enough for her not even to consider the journey. She had heard enough from Carey himself about the tough living conditions and the ravages of tropical disease. It would be hard to imagine, with William so absorbed and interested in sea voyages, that she would not have heard of the scurvy and the many deaths at sea. She probably hated the thought of having to be separated from her closely-knit family, the familiar food and climate. She probably also knew that going to India as a missionary was illegal.

I agree with Beck that, 'Dorothy's decision to stay was a sane and sensible choice rather than an insane and sinful one.'

After waiting for six weeks in the south of England and then being asked to leave the ship and told to wait for the Danish ship, Carey, eight-year-old Felix and Dr John Thomas showed up one day for breakfast with Dorothy, in a last-ditch effort to get her to change her mind. She remained adamant. Dr Thomas says he used fear to put pressure on her, saying that if she did not come with them she might never see her husband again. That, it seems, did it, and Dorothy relented, agreeing to accompany them to India, so long as her sister Kitty could go with her.

One can imagine how she felt, having just a few hours in which to pack, sort out her house, say good-bye to her family, knowing that she might never see them again if she were to succumb, as was likely, to sickness. Meanwhile, the men had to tell the appropriate committee at the Baptist Missionary Society about the change in plans, and make the arrangements for the money needed for their tickets.

They landed in Calcutta after a voyage of five months, in November 1793. It was cooler than normal. There was no one to welcome them or offer them hospitality; they were entering illegally. They were on their own.

Carey at once was preoccupied with putting into practice the Bengali he had learnt on the ship from Dr Thomas and preaching to the Bengalis. This was, after all, his passion and his life's goal.

Meanwhile Dorothy with three boys and a baby did not know the language and had to look after the children in this strange land with strange food and people who were always staring at her. It seems that Carey did not have much time for the family. Dorothy, with her sister, was largely left alone to care for and feed the family. Kitty was a great support. As were the Thomas family, but they were somewhat of a mixed blessing; financial mistakes resulted in his being hounded by his creditors.

Limited funds meant the families were housed poorly, in three separate dwellings in different parts of Calcutta. This in itself was unsettling. After five months, they were offered free land to develop in a tiger-haunted, malaria-infested jungle in South Bengal. It would have meant living in a hut – but an Englishman in a government house came to their rescue. The extreme heat and humidity along with many snakes kept Dorothy in constant fear for her children. She struggled with chronic and debilitating dysentery. Her one support, Kitty, then decided to marry Charles Short the man who had offered them his house. Dorothy now felt truly alone.

But their conditions were to change for the better. William was offered a manager's job in an indigo factory with a good salary and a secure house with servants. Very important too was the support of the Udnys – a godly family. But by this time Dorothy must have had enough, and in 1795 she took a turn for the worse. The last straw seems to have been the death of their five-year old son, Peter. Carey who was himself very sick, could not find a grave-digger, pallbearer or casket maker for their son. Isolated from other Christians or Europeans, Carey had to turn to the local Muslims to help him bury Peter – which was taboo for them. His domestic staff refused to touch even the poles of the coffin. To do so meant excommunication.

This was a very traumatic time for Carey and it seems for the first time he resorted to an uncustomary outburst of anger at those who threatened to ostracize the only people to whom he could turn for help.

With difficulty, he got four Muslims to dig the grave – with inevitable results. The local community excommunicated the four – who came and complained. Carey was now faced with a dilemma: should he stand with these men who had stood with him in his time of need? If he refused, he could expect no help in future. Gentle persuasion was not going to deliver reconciliation. Instead, Carey angrily sent two men to bring the Muslim leader to his house, by force if necessary, and kept him under virtual house arrest while a judge was fetched to settle the matter. He was made to eat with the excommunicants – or go hungry. Local traditions had pushed Carey to the limits of his own nature.

For Dorothy, grief at losing her child tipped her over the edge of sanity. She started losing touch with reality. She began to have delusions of Carey's infidelity and would follow him around to catch him red-handed. She would follow him to the factory and publicly accuse him in foul language, shouting obscenities and causing great embarrassment. She saw Carey as her enemy and sought to get rid of him, even taking a kitchen knife to him. She had to be confined to her room for her own safety and his for twelve years, until her death in 1807.

This was enough reason for Carey's biographers to dismiss her. But it was Dorothy's sacrifice which enabled Carey to do all that he did:

- had she refused to come to India, Carey would have been forced to return to England;
- had she come from an educated upper-class background she might have completely refused the poor life-style he had to accept during the early years, when mission support was not there;
- had she insisted on studying and ministering, they could not have looked after their children in the early years;
- as a result of her mental illness, mission societies began to treat wives as equally important as their husbands:

they were interviewed, their vision, abilities and mental health were examined, their needs and concerns provided for.
- Beck says that Dorothy became the hard anvil on which was hammered some of the success of Carey's remarkable career.

A beautiful marriage

As human beings made in the image of a Triune God we are made for fellowship and intimacy. Although Carey's decision to remarry a Danish countess just a few weeks after Dorothy's death in December 1807 was greeted by the community with some dismay, the 13 years that followed were Carey's most happy and productive. The community realized soon enough that for 12 years Carey had had a marriage in name only. There was also concern that the countess' physical disabilities might be as much a liability for Carey and the community as the mental disabilities they had had to deal with in Dorothy.

Dorothy had been confined for 12 years, two rooms away from Carey's study where he spent long hours. He would have heard her reproaches, her ranting and raving, and yet he had to carry on. Life without a soulmate would have made life very lonely. Yet he was able to accomplish all that he did and manage his children. The wives of their little community stood in as mother to the four boys.

It was only natural that Carey should remarry six months after being widowed. Charlotte Rumohr was a student of Carey's, learning English from him and also learning his faith. Hers was probably a lifeless Christian faith, but what she saw of this community's faith inspired her and she went on to take baptism from Carey. She lived next door to the Serampore community so was in close touch with them in spite of her disabilities. She could not walk or talk properly: a fire in her home in her early childhood had disabled her. Yet she had a cheerful spirit, in contrast to poor Dorothy who had known only the rigours and sickness of their early life in India.

Charlotte was well-read, refined and had come to India of her own choice. So it was easy for her to love and understand Carey who by now had probably realized that he had not spent enough time with Dorothy and the children. He was able to be a better husband to Charlotte. Charlotte was deeply interested in him and his work and was a real partner to him spiritually, linguistically and in his mission – she was particularly concerned about the education of Indian girls.

After her death Carey wrote, 'she had lived only for me. Her solicitude for my happiness was incessant and so certainly would she at all time interpret my looks, that any attempt to conceal anxiety or distress of mind would have been in vain'.

The following letter to Carey gives us a good feel of the tenderness of their relationship:

> My dearest love – I felt very much in parting with thee, and feel much in being so far from thee...I am sure thou wilt be happy and thankful on account of my voice, which is daily getting better, and thy pleasure greatly adds to mine own.
>
> I hope you will not think I am writing too often; I rather trust you will be glad to hear of me...the good state of my health, the freshness of the air, and the variety of objects enliven my spirits, yet I cannot help longing for you. Pray, my love, take care of your health that I may have the joy to find you well.
>
> I thank thee most affectionately, my dearest love, for thy kind letter. Though the journey is very useful to me, I cannot help feeling much to be so distant from you, but I am much with you in my thoughts...the Lord be blessed for the kind protection He has given to his cause in a time of need. May He still protect and guide and bless his dear cause, and give us all hearts growing in love and zeal...I felt very much

affected in parting with thee. I see plainly it would not do to go from you; my heart cleaves to you. I need not say (for I hope you know my heart is not insensible) how much I feel your kindness in not minding any expense for the recovery of my health. You will rejoice to hear me talk in my old way, and not in that whispering manner.

I feel so much pleasure in writing to you, my love, that I cannot help doing it. I was nearly disconcerted by Mrs. – laughing at my writing so often; but then, I thought, I feel so much pleasure in receiving your letters that I may hope you do the same.

I thank thee, my love, for thy kind letter.

One cannot help but feel glad for Carey that after 26 years he found fulfilment in his domestic life. His financial and domestic problems were now behind him. In 1813 Parliament had given permission for missionaries to go to India. Some young men did come to help the veteran missionaries. But they soon became headaches for the oldguards. Carey went through the conflicts with colleagues we all go through. One factor that sustained him through those years was the fact that there was now one person who loved him, believed in him, cared for him and sustained him.

Creative leisure

William Carey was an unusually rounded man. When he worked with his hands as a shoemaker, he cultivated his mind. Learning was a hobby. Later when he worked with his mind as a translator, he relaxed with his hands – in gardening and forestry.

Even as a child growing up in England in poverty, Drewery says, Carey

...displayed a passionate interest in his surroundings, particularly in plants and animals. If he had set his heart on obtaining any particular flower or insect for his collection, he was heedless of dirt or discomfort in the pursuit of it. His bedroom was filled with specimens, with birds and insects both alive and dead, which would indicate that his mother must have shown commendable tolerance of her son's enthusiasm.

Carey was primarily a cordwainer – a little more skilled than a shoemaker. His father Edmund was a weaver, later a schoolmaster and a parish clerk. Even though they were very poor, William's father planted in him the seeds of learning. Edmund had a special interest in the education of women when it was not considered important for women to be literate. He was a man of initiative and a model for William.

Carey had to stop his formal studies at twelve years of age to earn a living. He tried his hand as an agricultural labourer but his sensitive skin prevented him from being in the sun too long. Northampton was then an important place for shoemaking, so the obvious thing was to learn an indoor job. Carey joined Clarke Nichols as an apprentice. There his fellow apprentice John Warr was to take this sixteen-year-old boy to a meeting of Dissenters where he was converted.

It seems that as a shoemaker Carey kept both his hands and his mind active. It was probably there while making shoes that he thought up his sermons, and looked at his huge world map on which he had put information gleaned from his reading of Captain James Cook's voyages. Also he made a large leather map with all the countries of the world on it. His friends nicknamed him Columbus because of his fascination with sea voyages.

His thirst for knowledge was insatiable and led him to learn Greek on his own, just by asking another student for help and going through Mr Nichols' library. He was to learn Hebrew and Latin too, on his own initiative. He also had miles and miles to walk to sell his shoes – times when his mind was busy preparing sermons.

In England wherever he lived he managed to have a garden around his cottage. In India he continued with his botanical interests, putting his heart and soul into getting and growing plants. He had a huge, beautiful garden of which he was justly proud. He writes to a friend that he is

> passionately fond of nature and that I relax my mind from pursuits of a more laborious kind by attending thereto. My museum and garden are therefore not only sources of pleasure but of health to me.

His five-acre arboretum in Serampore had trees like eucalyptus, mahogany, deodar, teak and tamarind. These trees were unknown in Calcutta. By June 1880, just six months after arriving in Serampore, he was to tell William Roxburgh, his friend, of the 427 species of plants he had in his garden.

His youngest son Jonathan writes about his fathers powers of observation and his natural curiosity for all of God's creation. He says:

> In objects of nature my father was exceedingly curious. His collection of mineral ores, and other objects of natural history, was extensive, and obtained his particular attention in seasons of leisure and recreation. The science of botany was his constant delight and study; and his fondness for his garden remained to the last. No one was allowed to interfere in the arrangements of this his favourite retreat; and it is here he enjoyed his most pleasant moments of secret devotion and meditation. The arrangements made by him were on the Linnaean system; and to disturb the bed or border of his garden was to touch the apple of his eye. He had the best and rarest botanical collection of plants in the East, to the extension of which, by his correspondence with persons of eminence in Europe and other parts of the world his attention was constantly directed and in return he supplied his correspondents with rare collections from the East. It was painful to observe with what distress my father quitted this scene of

his enjoyments, when extreme weakness, during his last illness, prevented his going to his favourite retreat. Often when he was unable to walk, he was drawn into the garden in a chair placed on a board with four wheels.

His passion in obtaining botanic samples is revealed in his request to his son Jabez who was going as a missionary to Amboyna, Malay island. He says:

> Be sure to send me every possible vegetable production. Plant tubers and bulbs in a box so thickly as to touch one another, or hang them dry in a well-covered basket in an airy part of the ship. Send, if you can, two or three hundred of each sort. I shall be glad of the smallest as well as the largest common plants. Think none insignificant. Plant the small in boxes, and always keep some well-rooted and ready; if too recently planted, they die on the way. Just before dispatching them sow very thickly amongst them seeds of trees, fruits and shrubs, covered with a finger's thickness of fresh soil. They should be watered a little on the voyage. You must often send the same thing, as it will be ten to one that they arrive alive. So send abundant seeds of every sort, perfectly ripe and dry, in named paper packets, in a box or basket, secured from the rats; and, if possible, cite the due soil. Parasitical plants, such as you have seen me tie on trees, need only be stripped where they grow, and hung in baskets in an airy part of the ship, or even at the maintop. All boxes of plants must have strips of wood over them, to keep out the rats. Nothing must be put in the hold. Send me as many live birds as possible; also small quadrupeds, monkeys etc. Beetles, lizards, frogs, serpents may be put in a small keg of rum. I have much confidence in you to add greatly to my stock of natural productions. But you must persevere in both collecting and sending.

Just reading these instructions is exhausting, and yet this was Carey's leisure-time pursuit. He was not only a translator, a teacher, and a reformer but he was also a serious botanist.

He edited three volumes of his friend William

Roxburgh's *Flora Indica* which is still a standard work with botanists. In the title page of this major publication he wrote, 'All thy works praise thee, O Lord' – David.

In 1823 he was elected a fellow of the Linnaean Society of London. He also became a member of the Geological Society of London and a corresponding member of the Horticultural Society of London.

Beauty out of ashes

Carey was in Calcutta when Marshman broke the news to him – just when the printing and translation work was at its height – that a devastating fire had ravaged the hall which housed their printing press.

During the day this hall, which was 200ft long and 50ft feet wide, housed at least twenty *munshis* working on different translations, the type-founders, compositors, pressmen, binders and writers.

This huge fire had consumed Carey's manuscripts along with ten Bible translations. His translation of the epic *Ramayana* which he had translated along with Marshman was also gone. His huge project of the polyglot Sanskrit dictionary – his *magnum opus* – was now just ashes. Vast quantities of English paper, fourteen founts of Oriental types, new supplies of Hebrew, Greek and English type, priceless dictionaries, grammars, steel punches, deeds and account books of the property were all gone.

As Carey returned and surveyed the scene with the chaplain of Fort William, he said, with tears in his eyes,

> In one short evening the labours of years are consumed. How unsearchable are the ways of God. I had lately brought some things to the utmost perfection of which they seemed capable, and contemplated the missionary establishment with perhaps too much self-congratulation. The Lord has laid me low, that I may look more simply to him.

Thomason, an eyewitness writes:

> Who could stand in such a place, at such a time with such a man, without feelings of sharp regret and solemn exercise of mind. I saw the ground strewed with half-consumed paper, on which in the course of a very few months the words of life would have been printed. The misshapen lumps – the sad remains of beautiful types consecrated to the service of the sanctuary. All was smiling and promising a few hours before – now all is vanished into smoke or converted into rubbish. Return now to thy books, regard God in all thou doest. Let God be exalted in all thy plans and purposes and labours. He can do without thee.

Earlier he had been comforted by a colleague at Fort William College. 'However vexing it may be, a road the second time travelled is usually taken with more confidence and ease than at the first.'

This is exactly what Carey braced himself to do. He decided that the 'Phoenix arising anew from the ashes' might be a myth, but 'we have indeed been promised a crown of beauty, instead of ashes':

> The Spirit of the Sovereign Lord is on me, because the Lord has anointed me to preach good news to the poor. He has sent me to bind up the brokenhearted, to proclaim freedom for the captives and release from darkness for the prisoners, to proclaim the year of the Lord's favor and the day of vengeance of our God, to comfort all who mourn, and provide for those who grieve in Zion – to bestow on them a crown of beauty instead of ashes, the oil of gladness instead of mourning, and a garment of praise instead of a spirit of despair. They will be called oaks of righteousness, a planting of the Lord for the display of his splendour. They will rebuild the ancient ruins and restore the places long devastated; they will renew the ruined cities that have been devastated for generations (Isaiah 61:1–4).

Carey resolved that he would take God's word at its face value, that from those ashes, he would have a better press and more scholarly translations. They were able to salvage the five presses, punches and matrices.

And within a few months, Ward had already opened out a long warehouse nearer the river shore.

Little did these simple scholars know that this fire would prove to be the means of making them and their work famous all over Europe and America as well as in India. In just 50 days about ten thousand pounds were raised in England and Scotland alone, until Andrew Fuller, Carey's friend, supporter and a BMS leader, returning from his last fund-raising campaign, entered the room of his committee, declaring, 'We must stop the contributions.' More money had been raised than was needed to cover the losses of the fire. Even in America people helped generously. In Calcutta the newspapers caught the enthusiasm, and one leading article concluded with the assurance that the Serampore press would, 'like a phoenix of antiquity, rise from its ashes, winged with new strength and destined, in a lofty and long enduring flight, widely to diffuse the benefits of knowledge throughout the East'.

After two months Fuller in England was able to send slips of sheets of the Tamil Testament, printed from these types, to the towns and churches which had subscribed. After six months the whole loss in Oriental types was recovered. Carey and his two heroic brethren wrote: 'We found on making the trial that the advantages of going over the same ground a second time were so great that they fully counter-balanced the time requisite to be devoted thereto in a second translation. The fire, the cause of which was never discovered, and insurance against which did not exist in India, had given birth to revised editions.'

Another result was that two new missionaries arrived in Serampore – one professional type-cutter and the other a doctor with his wife perhaps the first missionary nurse.

This doctor was soon to be deported (because neither had licenses from the East India Company) just weeks before the debate on the renewal of the East India Company's Charter was to be debated in Parliament. Wilberforce tirelessly campaigned with petitions about letting missionaries go to India. In June 1813 the Charter Renewal Bill was amended and included a clause stating that it was the duty of Britain 'to promote the interest and happiness' of the Indian people by 'taking such measures . . . as may tend to the moral improvement' and that 'facilities should be afforded by law to persons wishing to go to India for that purpose'. The first person to be granted that license was Carey's nephew Eustace.

Trouble never strikes singly: the fire had come after a huge earthquake, and deaths in each of the seven missionary families at Serampore. Carey had himself just buried a grandson. Yet Marshman writes to Ryland in England, in an SOS:

> The calamity was another leaf of the ways of Providence, calling for the exercise of faith in Him, whose word, firm as the pillars of Heaven, has decreed that all things work together for good to them that love God. Be strong therefore in the Lord. He will never forsake the work of His own hands.

Conflicts in community

Another fire was to burn the heart of Carey and that was the fire of contention with his society in England, coupled with that of the younger missionaries who had joined him. This bitterness originated in England.

Forbes Jackson says that the greatest trial of a missionary is often another missionary. This was the case with the five very able and dedicated men who came to Serampore to assist Carey but who temporarily split and started the Calcutta Missionary Union. Carey says that never in his life – and he had more than his share of distresses – 'had anything preyed so much upon his spirit as this episode'.

This happened at a time when Carey had been grieved by the great loss of his second wife who had brought greatest comfort in his life. He had just lost his father, and also broken a leg. His son Felix had brought great humiliation and embarrassment to him. Felix had been sent to Burma and now had come to Calcutta behaving as though he were the ambassador from Burma. He had delusions of grandeur and began drinking heavily and adopting a lavish lifestyle. Carey eventually had to repay all the debts that his son incurred.

Carey's colleague, Ward, was worn out and in poor health. Marshman was being attacked by the younger missionaries for being autocratic. All three men were feeling the strain of many years in the debilitating climate of Bengal with no home-leave, vacation or relief.

The so-called 'pious clause' inserted in the 1813 Charter of the East India Company by Wilberforce to increase missionary activity and thereby create greater freedom, brought increased bickering and internal conflicts.[1]

Dr. Johns, who had been deported just a few months before Wilberforce's Parliamentary victory, criticized Marshman for not trying hard enough to have him stop being deported. This charge emerged just when others were planning to come out to India. False allegations take their toll: this one coloured the perspective of the newcomers.

---

[1] The 'pious clause' in the 1813 Charter of the East India Company was Wilberforce's undertaking, drafted by Charles Grant. It sought to ease the way for chaplains and ministers of religion to India. The preamble read: 'That it is the peculiar and bounden duty of the legislature to promote by all just and prudent means the interests and happiness of the inhabitants of the British Dominions in India, and for these ends such measures ought to be adopted as may gradually tend to their advancement in useful knowledge, and to their religious and moral improvement.'

This happened to have been the time when the Mission society was growing rapidly. Two of the 'old trio' in England– Sutcliff and Fuller – had died (the third member being Dr. John Ryland). They had known Carey personally, encouraged him with letters, with money and coordinated their mission. Nineteen new members had joined the society. They did not know Carey personally. They had not been associated with the growingpains of the mission; they did not know why the oldguard did things the way they did them.

Out of the three, Andrew Fuller had been the most faithful supporter and friend to Carey and the Mission. This chief apologist of missions had worn himself out to see that the new Charter had the 'pious clause' put in it. He prayed for, raised money, preached, and wrote encouraging letters to Carey. Fuller maintained all along that Serampore should be self-governing, because the field staff were better able to govern themselves than the Home Board could govern them from England – at a time when letters took about six months to arrive.

The Mission had become self-supporting because Marshman's schools generated income. This they ploughed back into the missionary work. All along Carey was also giving to the Mission from his income in Calcutta. With this self-sufficiency naturally came a fair bit of independence.

The Mission in the field had become famous, while its Home Board's control had weakened. This was inevitable given the field-workers' greater age and experience of India. They knew what would work and what would not, and they knew their own strengths and limitations better than the Board at home.

So when the new missionaries were leaving for India – with glasses that had been coloured by Dr Johns – the Home Board was also complaining about its lack of control over Serampore. Misunderstandings lasted for 15 years. People doubted the integrity of the Serampore missionaries and suspected them of misappropriating funds. This in spite of Carey giving all he had to missions, so much so that he writes that, 'If I were to die today, I should not leave property enough for the purchase of a coffin and my wife would be entirely unprovided for.'

Carey himself gives an amplified translation of the charges thus:

> The Serampore Missionaries – Carey, Marshman and Ward – have acted a dishonest part, alias are rogues. But we do not include Dr. Carey in this charge of dishonesty; he is an easy sort of a man, who will agree to anything for the sake of peace, or in other words he is a fool. Mr. Ward it is well known, say they, was the tool of Dr. Marshman, but it is gone from the present scene, and it is unlovely to say any evil of the dead.

The crisis came to a head when the committee demanded that all the property at Serampore – schools, printing press, church, and houses – be transferred to the trustees; to which the Serampore trio refused. This further fuelled the suspicions of the committee. Then the committee was to send a printer to assist Ward whom they directed to stay at Serampore – but being a closely-knit family, the missionaries resented this. They preferred to see if the person would fit in with their community over a period of time. Next came Eustace Carey, Carey's nephew, who at first was very appreciative of the work of his uncle, but later became critical because of the committee's reports. He also thought the pioneering missionaries too rigid and autocratic.

The schism it seems was complete when the younger group formed the Calcutta Missionary Union. About this Carey writes,

> I do not recollect in my whole life anything which has given me so much distress as this schism. Many sleepless nights have I spent examining what we have done to give it occasion

but can discover nothing on which I can fix. The Mission, however, is rent in twain, and exhibits the scandalous appearance of a body divided against itself.

When asked to join the 'Union' and leave Marshman out, Carey said that he was quite aware of Marshman's faults but his excellences were such that his defects were almost concealed by them. He said that he despised all attempts to draw him away from his colleague of 18 years. He was very willing to remove misunderstanding; he would on bended knee ask pardon of anyone he had offended; 'that if it was proved that I had either said or done what was wrong, I should count it an honour to acknowledge it, and would do it without hesitation'.

His humility, loyalty to his old friends, patience with the younger men, and the deep desire for unity, paid off when finally, in 1820, there was reconciliation. The efforts of the older and the younger missionaries became tributaries which joined to form one big river of blessing to many states.

In the face of the devastating floods of 1823 Carey showed characteristic and dogged perseverance, a quality he displayed throughout his life in the face of every conceivable discouragement – of which he had more than his share. His school buildings were seriously damaged, his own home destroyed and his beautiful garden washed away. But now, unlike in 1812 after the fire, there was no help forthcoming from England. Slander had stifled the generosity of the Baptists at home towards the work in Serampore. His own sisters who were very close to him for a time, turned against him. His son Jabez too was to join the opposition briefly.

After 16 years of this bitter wrangling, the trio were in abject poverty. No longer was Carey a teacher at Fort William; the Serampore College and Mission lost all their Indian funds through the collapse of the European Agency Houses they had in Bengal (established for trading and banking). The economic depression of the 1820s reduced trade. But the trio were not so much concerned about their personal needs as for the 19 mission stations that they had to maintain plus other financial commitments Carey had to his family in England. As always in time of distress, the missionaries accepted their plight as a sign of God's chastening.

For two months the 19 mission stations did not get their allowances and at last Carey sent home an appeal for financial support. It could be that these anxieties helped Carey and Marshman to surrender their independence and fall in line with the wishes of the home committee. All the Serampore properties were transferred to the care of 11 trustees in England. All they asked was that they be allowed to stay rent-free for the remainder of their lives. Their plea did not go unheeded; the society sent them a thousand pounds in 1831. Then John Mack re-joined them and this brought great cheer and encouragement.

Carey was now very ill with a fever that lasted a month: his healing came not just from the finances and the presence of John Mack, but from letters that came which were for the first time in years gracious and kind.

William Carey died three years later, on 9 June 1834. Robert Hall spoke thus of him:

> That extraordinary man, who from the lowest obscurity and poverty, without assistance, rose by dint of unrelenting industry to the highest honours of literature, became one of the first of Orientalists, the first of missionaries and the instrument of diffusing more religious knowledge among his contemporaries than has fallen to the lot of any individual since the Reformation; a man who unites with the most profound and varied attainments the fervour of an evangelist, the piety of a saint and the simplicity of a child.

4

William Carey and the Modernization of India

We turn in this chapter to some of the profound contributions of William Carey, and those contemporaries who shared his beliefs, to the process of modernization in India. Some historians believe that the modernization of India began on the March 7, 1835. On that date Lord Thomas Babington Macaulay advocated in his famous 'Minute On Education', that the East India Company ought to use its grant for Public Instruction, for English education.

If, however, we begin to ask simple questions such as, Who was Macaulay? Who and what influenced his decision? What enabled him to overrule the great Orientalists who advocated teaching of Sanskrit, Persian, and Arabic? Why was this money available in the first place? What exactly did he mean by 'English' education? How did he foresee his Minute being carried out? we would quickly come to the conclusion that his Minute actually was the culmination of a process started in 1792.

Carey's contributions to modernization have not been adequately appreciated. Sadly, some scholars even undermine them. The process of India's reform has already been halted, and in some important respects Indian society seems to be reverting to its old evils. We must look not so much at Carey himself, but at the beliefs he shared with others that led to the reforms being initiated.

But first we need to be rid of the idea that India's contact with England automatically resulted in reform, an idea rooted not in the evidence of history, but in a blind faith in the doctrine of Social Evolution which wrongly holds that societies inevitably evolve and improve.

We need also to get a bird's eye-view of the people and processes that lay behind the reforms.

The British temper towards India at the time of Carey

Almost until the arrival of Lord William Bentinck in 1828 as the Governor General, which symbolized the Evangelical take-over of the East India Company, the mainstream British attitude toward India did not favour a struggle for its improvement; involvement in India should be kept to a minimum.

This view was shaped by three major interests.

For the Directors of The East India Company, India was simply a trading base. Most of them did not even want to govern India, let alone assume the responsibility of reforming it. Their simple commercial minds found Lord Wellesley's empire-building military successes, for example, too much for their ledgers and Wellesley was recalled.

Lord Macaulay, an outstanding historian of the nineteenth century, described the East India Company during the initial phase of its rule in Bengal as 'a gang of public robbers'. Clive, who won Bengal for the Company, had himself taken a bribe of two hundred thousand pounds from the puppet he installed as the Nawab. The Company's greed was a major factor which, within the first 50 years of its power, helped destroy India's two thousand year-old economic strength. This strength had been built on trade and industry, especially the weaving industry. Casteism had ensured that the benefits of the economy did not percolate down to the average person, who therefore had little interest in defending the socio-economic system when it was attacked by foreigners.

For the British military men such as Clive and Wellesley, India was primarily so much 'territory to be conquered'. It was an attitude which ensured that even though Lord Wellesley was convinced of the rightness of Carey's campaign against *sati* in 1806, he did not issue an edict against it, as Bentinck later did in 1829.

The British intellectuals and humanitarians in India such as Sir Thomas Munro and Sir John Malcolm tended merely to respect and romanticize the 'customs and wisdom of the natives'. The British Orientalists patronized Sanskrit and rediscovered the greatness of the ancient Indian literature, which helped to revive the self-respect of the Indian élite. Their efforts, however, could do nothing to reform the populace of India. On the contrary it appeared that they were reinforcing the religious basis for some of the social evils. Raja Ram Mohun Roy – himself a great Sanskrit Scholar – severely condemned the attempt of the British Orientalists to start a Sanskrit College in Calcutta, which would have further solidified the existing class distinctions.

For decades the British had a policy of not employing Indians for responsible administrative positions. They believed that Indians were dishonest and could not be trusted. Although both Munro and Malcolm also agreed that Indians were dishonest, they nevertheless argued against this policy of discriminating against Indians. They thought that if the Indian élite were paid on a par with the British, they too might become morally upright. Nonetheless, they ruled out the possibility that Indians could be reformed, Sir Thomas Munro, Governor of Madras from 1820–24, wrote on June 30, 1821:

> I have no faith in the modern doctrine of the rapid improvement of the Hindoos, or of any other people. The character of the Hindoos is probably much the same as when Vasco

da Gama first visited India, and it is not likely that it will be much better a century hence.

When I read, as I sometimes do, of a measure by which a large province had been suddenly improved, or a race of semi-barbarians, civilized, almost to quakerism, I throw away the book.

A minority with a missionary vision

Those reformers who advocated this 'modern doctrine of the rapid improvement of the Hindoos' were the Fourth Force in England. They were only a tiny minority at the end of the eighteenth century, but, in contrast to the other three viewpoints, they argued for a maximum possible British involvement in India in the mutual interest of both England and India.

It should be obvious that the reformation and the modernization of India had to be a work, primarily, of those who both loved India and were not blind to its faults. A reformer has to have some basis for believing that even the most degenerate person can be saved; some basis for hope that good can triumph over evil, that a whole society, oppressed by ignorance and 'wickedness' for thousands of years, could be transformed, almost miraculously, without the use of force.

The power of two pens

Let us look briefly at two books and their authors who began the modernization of India. One, Charles Grant, worked behind the scenes in England, while the other, William Carey, laboured in the heat and dust of India.

These reformers began to articulate their views one year before the British Parliament was to renew the Charter of the East India Company in 1793.

Charles Grant had served in the East India Company

for 13 years in India and had seen the evils both of the Company and of India's populace. He believed that both needed to be changed.

William Carey gathered his knowledge of the world and of India from a careful study of history and from the reports of travellers such as Captain Cook.

Carey's book was written in 1791 and published in 1792. Grant's was written in 1792 and published in 1797, and, even before it was published, managed to influence the Parliamentary Debate on India of 1793. After his book was reprinted as a State Paper in 1812, it became the then most widely read statement on India. By then Grant was both a Member of Parliament and one of the top brass of the East India Company.

Charles Grant's Observations

Grant's book, which began to influence reformers' minds, including that of Lord Macaulay's father, had an elongated title: *Observations on the State of Society among the Asiatic Subjects of Great Britain, particularly with respect to Morals and on the Means of Improving it. Written Chiefly in the Year 1792.*

Grant was a member of the famous Evangelical group, 'The Clapham Sect'. He was a close friend of its leader, William Wilberforce – the Evangelical member of Parliament who was then fighting a battle that was to last till the end of his life against the British law that allowed its Chartered companies to buy and to sell African slaves.

Charles Grant began to look at India differently from the way his colleagues in the East India Company viewed the colony, primarily because he was converted to Evangelical Christianity in 1790, two years before he wrote his book.

The word 'conversion' has come to acquire negative connotations because of the belief that all truth is *relative*, and all beliefs valid. In England, in Grant's day, changing one's religion or religious beliefs was not the primary meaning of conversion. According to the Evangelicals, every baptized person, called 'Christian', also needed to be converted, i.e., needed to repent of sin and be transformed by the power of the Holy Spirit, through faith in Jesus Christ. (The word 'Evangelical' was initially used for those Anglicans who believed the Bible to be God's word, and emphasized the necessity of personal conversion. Later, the word began to be used to describe all Christians who shared that belief.)

For Grant himself, to be converted meant that even though he was a businessman, he no longer lived for making money, but for honouring the Lord Jesus Christ. That, in turn, meant that he could no longer look at the Indian people with the eyes of a merchant – a people to be exploited for economic gain – but instead, he looked from Christ's perspective: Indians had to be loved and served, as Jesus would have done. An interesting and tangible proof of Grant's conversion is that upon his death in 1824 he left his legacy for William Carey. All the wealth he had earned from India through the East India Company was reinvested in the modernization of India. The sincerity of his heart is also authenticated by the fact that his son, also named Charles Grant, put his reforming ideas into the 1833 Charter of the East India Company. His other son, Robert Grant who also went back to serve India composed the famous hymn, 'O worship the King, all glorious above.'

In order to be converted, Grant had to acknowledge and then repent of the sin in his own life. It meant he could neither overlook the evil habits of the people of India nor excuse them. As a practical man of commerce (unlike many theoreticians of today), he realized that moral poverty could cause a great country to sink into chronic misery.

Upon the whole, then, we cannot avoid recognizing in the people of Hindostan, a race of men lamentably degenerate and base; retaining but a feeble sense of moral obligation...governed by malevolent and licentious passions, strongly exemplifying the effects produced on society by a great and general corruption of manners, and sunk in misery by their vices, in a country peculiarly calculated by its natural advantages, to promote the prosperity of its inhabitants.

William Carey's Enquiry

Many people today understandably detest the very title of Carey's *An Enquiry Into The Obligations Of Christians To Use Means For The Conversion Of The Heathen.* The words 'heathen' and 'conversion' have acquired negative and repulsive connotations.

However, all the great social reformers in nineteenth century India accepted Carey's belief that in many cases, conversion – or change of one's character and false beliefs – was the only effective means of social reform. The proliferation of new religious sects that followed Carey testifies to the compelling power of Carey's conviction. The better known examples are: The *Brahmo Samaj* (Ram Mohun Roy), the *Prarthna Samaj* (Keshub Chandra Sen), the *Satya Shodhak Samaj* (Jotiba Phule), the *Arya Samaj* (Swami Dayanand) and the Ramakrishna Mission (Vivekananda) which is still fighting a legal battle demanding that it should be classified as a separate religion and not considered Hindu. This belief that conversion is a key to reform continued well into this century, at least until 1956 when Dr B. R. Ambedkar converted to Buddhism with his half-a-million followers. The reasons for the perceived connection between conversion and reform will become clear shortly.

If you read Carey's *Enquiry* you will find that Carey was inquiring into the question of whether or not Christians were under an obligation (in the light of the commands of the Lord Jesus Christ) to help transform societies that live in intellectual, moral, social, political, and spiritual darkness.

We have pointed out that we cannot even think of reforming a society unless we first acknowledge it to be needing reform, however sophisticated a name we choose to give to a society in the grip of moral decadence. For example, militant Hindu forces fighting for a *Ram Rajya*, are implicitly acknowledging that India is a kingdom of a demon-god – Ravana.[1] During Carey's time, such aspirations warranted the adjective 'heathen'.

Carey was recognized as a 'friend of India', yet he saw no problem in using the word 'heathen'. It was the word an educated Englishman used in a descriptive rather than a derogatory sense. Today we would describe India with phrases such as 'third world', 'under-developed' or 'a developing country'; where we now see things in economic and technological terms alone, Carey saw the moral and philosophical roots of economic backwardness. As a matter of fact the Economists perceived themselves primarily as moral philosophers. Adam Smith's work, for example, implied that the British Government in India submit an annual report entitled 'Moral and Material Progress in India'.

How can a society be transformed morally?

Carey did not agree with the humanitarians such as Sir Munro that the improvement of the morals of the people of 'Hindostan' was impossible. He believed, in obedience

---

[1] *Ram Rajya* is the mythical kingdom of the god-king *Rama*, where *dharma* or the Hindu idea of righteousness prevailed, and where each one performed the duties of their caste. The postmodern Hindu political party, the Bharatiya Janata Party (BJP) has been trying to turn India from a secular to a Hindu state, in the hope of establishing the *Ram Rajya*.

to Christ's command to 'go into all the world and preach the good news' of salvation: that reform, even dramatic improvement, was possible because God wanted to save human beings from their bondage to sin and Satan.

Carey's belief in the possibility of reform was rooted in his careful study of history – both biblical and secular. The second section of the *Enquiry*, for example, refers to an impressive list of well-documented stories of Christian preachers and missionaries who were his models. These include Peter, Paul, and the other apostles in the first century; Justin Martyr in the middle of the second century; Irenaeus around 170 AD; Tertullian 20 years later; Frumentius at the time of Constantine; Moses in 372; Palladius in 432; Austin in 596; Amandus in 589; Egidius in 648; Willifred in 684; Chilianus in 688; Charlemagne in 800; Ansgarius in 833; Methodius in 861; Wycliffe in 1369, followed by Huss, Jerome, Luther, Calvin, Melanchthon and Bucer, all of whose works led to the great European Reformation. Then there were Elliot in 1632; Brainerd in 1743; Ziegenbalg in 1706; and, finally, of course, Wesley, the impact of whose preaching had saved England from a bloody revolution such as the one in France, which, for Carey's readers, needed no documentation; for the French Revolution was happening as he wrote.

William Carey knew first-hand what social scientists such as Max Weber later documented, that politically and economically strong countries (such as Germany, Switzerland, Holland, and England) had been transformed by the preaching of reformers such as Martin Luther and John Calvin. Carey reasoned that what God could do for once barbarous Britons and for the once heathen Europe, he was able to accomplish anywhere. As he wrote in his *Enquiry*:

> The uncivilized state of the heathen, instead of affording an objection *against* preaching the Gospel to them, ought to furnish an argument *for* it. Can we as men, or as Christians,

hear that a great part of our fellow creatures, whose souls are as immortal as ours, and who are as capable as us...are enveloped in ignorance and barbarism? Can we hear that they are without the Gospel, without government, without laws, and without arts and sciences, and not exert...ourselves to introduce amongst them the sentiments of men, and of Christians? Would not the spread of the Gospel be the most effectual means of their civilization? Would not that make them useful members of society? We know that such effects did in a measure follow the afore-mentioned efforts of Elliot, Brainerd, and others amongst the American Indians...

Three presuppositions of Carey's reforms

It is easy to miss seeing, or to misunderstand, some basic assumptions of Carey's work, because the mentality of our day is so different from his.

First, today in a country such as India, every champion of the poor or the downtrodden sees himself as a saviour or a mini-messiah. Carey, in contrast, did not see himself as a saviour. For him, salvation was God's work. A reformer's primary duty was to pray. He wrote: 'One of the first, and most important of those duties which are incumbent upon us, is *fervent and united prayer.*'

This understanding that transforming mankind was the work of God sounds alien today, but for 150 years it remained Carey's abiding legacy to all the reformers of India, not only for the Christian but also his Hindu successors – from Raja Ram Mohun Roy at the beginning of the nineteenth century, to Mahatma Gandhi who was assassinated in a prayer meeting.

While many of the Indian reformers did not accept Carey's Trinitarian God, most of them, however, were forced to believe in a theistic God who is infinite-personal and Sovereign and is active in human history – one who answers prayers. These reformers recognized that neither the impersonal Deity of philosophic Hinduism, nor the finite gods of folk Hinduism were adequate for the needs of human societies. The former could not respond to prayers and the latter – gods and goddesses of mythology – were subject to the same human failings as ourselves. Carey believed that prayer makes a difference, not just in our minds but also in our history, because that was the essence of the Gospel: in Jesus the Messiah, the Sovereign Lord had entered human history as the 'Light of the world'.

His second assumption was that creation was rational, not magical or mystical. He placed great emphasis on introducing modern science to India. He himself taught Zoology, Botany, and Astronomy in his college at Serampore, besides, of course, Theology.

Some Indian intellectuals are espousing postmodernism because it seems to vindicate the traditional Hindu rejection of rational order, initially propagated by the Adi Shankaracharya. This revival of anti-rational religion in India undermines the scientific temper which reformers, beginning with Carey, tried to plant.

For our purposes here it is sufficient to point out that Carey spent enormous energy in translating and promoting the Bible, because, as a modern man, he believed that God's revelation alone could remove superstition and inculcate a confidence in human rationality – a prerequisite for the modernization of India.

Our generation has also tried to banish a third basic idea of Carey's, which was central to his understanding of how lasting reforms can take place: his concept of *conversion*. Two factors need to be understood here.

William Carey shared Charles Grant's belief that our moral rebellion is at the root of our human problems. Human misery is neither a result of *Avidhya* (ignorance of our divinity), nor is it a product of *karma* (desire). It is a result of human refusal to live under the moral authority of our heavenly Father.

Carey believed that it is the duty of reformers to share with everyone the blessings of 'conversion', of renewed fellowship with God. According to his study of history, conversion, reform, and modernization were intimately related processes.

Carey believed that by preaching and by translating and publishing the Bible in Indian vernaculars, he was laying the foundation stone for the modernization of India.

There is a second profound (and still relevant) factor which made Carey see conversion as the basis of reform. According to the British political doctrine of Religious Liberty, the State was not allowed to interfere with the religious conscience of the people. If social evils, such as untouchability, were results of religious beliefs, then they had to be countered by true and better beliefs – not by legislation, or administrative force. Some of the greatest Indian minds of the nineteenth century understood and appreciated the missionary effort to 'convert' Indians. This is how Keshub Chandra Sen, the successor of Raja Ram Mohun Roy and the founder of the *Prarthna Samaj*, reacted to the missionary work:

> We breathe, think, feel, move in a Christian atmosphere under the influence of Christian education; the whole mature society is awakened, enlightened, reformed...our hearts have been touched, conquered, subjugated by a superior power and that power is Christ. Christ rules British India, and not the British Government. England has sent us a tremendous moral force, in the life and character of that mighty prophet, to conquer and hold this vast empire. None but Jesus ever deserved this bright, precious diadem – India – and Christ shall have it.

The British Government, of course, had not sent the missionaries; but the Evangelicals needed to reform the East India Company and the British Parliament before they could get permission for their task of reforming India.

Reforming the British Parliament

The influence these Evangelicals exerted on Britain was much greater than in India. Within England they were better understood; their motives were less suspect, and their efforts were backed by thousands of unknown and unsung clergymen. What they had hoped to achieve in India is, two centuries later, still incomplete, substantially because Secular Humanism undermined what the Christians were seeking to do.

William Wilberforce was the chief spokesman for Grant and Carey inside the British Parliament. He forcefully presented their arguments that England must assume the responsibility of 'uplifting' India and believed that the chief problem of India's people was immorality and superstition in the guise of religion.

The doctrine of Religious Liberty had already come to have two implications: one was that the power of the State should not be used to tamper with the religious conscience of the people. If a social evil such as untouchability, or destructive superstitions such as astrology had overt religious sanction, then the State could not erase them by force or by legislation.

The other implication of the doctrine of Religious Liberty was that the removal of these religiously-sanctioned evils had to be the work of counter/reforming religious (or non-religious) ideas. All ideas had to be given the freedom to compete in the market of ideas to change people's beliefs and, thereby, their society.

Wilberforce argued that England should send Christian missionaries who could help 'improve' Indian society. In 1793 he succeeded in pushing his proposals through the House of Commons, but unfortunately, the House of Lords overthrew his proposals. In spite of this official rejection, Carey's sense of a divine call gave him the inner strength to set out for India in that same year.

It took 20 years of successful field work by Carey in India, lobbying within the East India Company by Charles Grant, and magnificent political work by Wilberforce in England, to persuade the Parliament in 1813 (when the Charter came up for renewal) to begin to assume its moral obligation to India.

William Carey's persistence paid off when William Wilberforce, whose proposals had failed in the British Parliament a second time in 1795, once again took up the issue in 1813. This time Wilberforce was backed by the documentation that had been supplied by Carey and others, such as Rev Claudius Buchanan – the Vice-Provost of Fort William College. These facts included lists of widows who had committed s*ati*. Wilberforce had made a practice of reading out their names at his dining table and praying for India. On 22 June, 1813 Wilberforce argued before Parliament:

> Christianity, independently of its effects on a future state of existence (i.e. heaven), has been acknowledged even by avowed skeptics, to be, beyond all other institutions that ever existed, favourable to the temporal interests and happiness of man: and never was there a country where there is a greater need than in India for the diffusion of its genial influence.

He continued his arguments on the first and twelfth of July:

> Let us endeavour to strike our roots into the soil by the gradual introduction and establishment of our own principles and opinions; of our laws, institutions, and manners; above all, as the source of every other improvement, of our religion, and consequently of our morals.

Wilberforce said that such a reforming effort, and not brute military force or political intrigue, would tie India to England with bonds of eternal gratitude.

The critics suggested that through his advocacy of

allowing missionaries to propagate Christianity in India, Wilberforce was counselling compulsory conversion. He rebutted the charge:

> Compulsion and Christianity! Why the very terms are at variance with each other – the ideas are incompatible. In the language of Inspiration itself, Christianity has been called the 'law of liberty'.

We should note two facts about the idea of religious pluralism. First, it was this commitment to the doctrine of the religious neutrality of the State which shaped Carey's arguments against *sati* in 1805–1806. The crux of his argument was that *sati* was not a religious practice enjoined by the Hindu scriptures. It could therefore be banned by the Government without violating the principle of separation of religion and state. A decade later, Raja Ram Mohun Roy was to use the same argument – since the only defence of the pro-*sati* lobby was that *sati* was a religious practice. It should also be noted that it was this spirit of administrative tolerance towards socio-religious practices, even when they were obviously evil, which later became the basis of the policy of religious pluralism of Independent India. Pluralism, another feature of modernization, is also under a serious threat today as India turns away from the legacy of the reformers.

Carey's generation, in contrast to our own, believed that it was possible for us to know truth because God had revealed it: in nature, in history and also in the Bible. Carey was committed to pluralism . . . to the idea that the state should not support one religious belief over another. He believed that it was the responsibility of the individual to discover the revealed truth – both in the scientific and historical spheres, as well as in the theological sphere. For example, is it true that some people are born Untouchables because of their *karma*, or is it a lie, perpetuated by a class of people in their own self-interest?

They believed that it was necessary for us to freely dialogue and debate truth, because we all tend to believe rationalizations that are untrue. Freedom of conscience is incomplete without the freedom to change one's beliefs, i.e. convert. A state that hinders conversion is uncivilized because it restricts the human quest for truth and reform.

In politics, arguments alone are rarely enough. William Wilberforce had already tasted defeat in Parliament more than once. In 1813 he took the precaution of mobilizing public pressure, particularly pressure on the House of Lords. The unsuspecting Lords were swept off their feet by the strength of public opinion. Historians acknowledge that public opinion, on which Wilberforce capitalized, was substantially a result of the publicity Carey's work had generated in England during the previous two decades. The impact of his work was greatly reinforced by books by Grant. Buchanan's well-received book, *The Christian Researches in Asia*, gave a vivid first-hand account of the horrors associated with the Jagganath festival in Puri.[2]

---

[2] The horrors of the Jagganath festival – anglicised to *Juggernaut* – are vividly described by C Buchanan in his *Christian Researches in Asia*, (quoted by V Mangalwadi in *Missionary Conspiracy: Letters to a Postmodern Hindu*.)

Budruck, Orissa, May 30, 1806. 'We know that we are approaching Juggernaut (and yet we are more than fifty miles from it) by the human bones which we have seen for some days strewed by the way. At this place we have been joined by several large bodies of pilgrim, perhaps 2,000 in number, who have come from various parts of Northern India. Some of them, with whom I have conversed, say, that they have been two months, on their march, travelling slowly in the honest season of the year, with their wives and children. Some old persons are among them who wish to die at Juggernaut. Numbers of pilgrims die on the road; and their bodies generally remain unburied. On a plain by the river, near the Pilgrim' s Caravanserai at this place, there are more than a hundred skulls. The dogs, jackals, and vultures, seem to live here on human prey. The vultures exhibit a shocking tameness. The obscene animals will not leave the body sometimes till we come close to them. This Budruck is a horrible place. Wherever I turn my eyes, I meet death in some shape or other. Surely' Juggernaut cannot be worse than Budruck.'

For India, two immediate positive results of this Parliamentary victory were: (a) the East India Company had to allow missionaries freedom to work, and (b) the Company was asked to earmark Rs.100,000 annually from its profits for public education in India. The consequence of the former was that great missionary educators, such as Alexander Duff, could freely come to India and open schools and colleges; while the consequence of the latter was Macaulay's Minute, 22 years later, which determined how this money, available since 1813, was to be used.

It took another 20 years of struggle (to the time of the next renewal of the Company's Charter in 1833), before the reformers' viewpoint really began to determine British policy. But the foundations had been laid.

Reforming the Company

Charles Grant knew that the greatest obstacle to the missionary endeavour to help reform India was his own East India Company. The Company, in turn, knew (partly from Grant's own writing, and also from the headache Wilberforce was giving to the Company's counterpart in Africa),

---

(Footnote 2 continued)

Juggernaut, 18 June, 1806: 'I have returned home from witnessing a scene which I shall never forget. At twelve o'clock of this day, being the great day of the feast, the Moloch of Hindostan was brought out of his temple amidst acclamations of hundreds of thousands of his worshippers...the throne of the idol was placed on a stupendous car or tower, about sixty feet in height, resting on wheels which indented the ground deeply, as they mined slowly under the ponderous machine. Attached to it were six cables, of the size and length of a ship's cable, by which the people drew it along. . . After the tower had proceeded some way, a pilgrim announced that he was ready to offer himself a sacrifice to the idol. He laid himself down in the road before the tower, as it was moving along, lying on his face, with his arm stretched forwards. The multitude passed round him, leaving the space clear, and he was crushed to death by the wheels of the tower. A shorn of joy was raised to the god. He is said to *smile* when the libation of that the missionaries would disturb the Company's profitable activities by exciting the natives. Carey, for example, was known to be a potential trouble-maker. While still in England he had been opposed even to using the sugar made by slave labour and imported by British companies.

Grant resolved to attempt the reform of the East India Company by becoming the leader of the reformers' assault on the Company's board. His first victory came in 1805–6 when he managed to send five 'serious' (reform-minded, Evangelical) clergymen to India as chaplains for the Company, to try to reform its employees. One of these five was the renowned Henry Martyn who spent his first months in India with Carey, and, under his influence, went on to create Hindustani as a modern literary language through his translation of the New Testament. It was the Hindustani created by Henry Martyn, Rev Gilchrist and the others at Fort William College, out of which came the modern Hindi and Urdu – the national languages of India and Pakistan.

Grant's victory, in a substantial measure, was a result of Carey's success in India. In 1800, Lord Wellesley had already been forced to invite Carey to teach Bengali to the administrators of the Company in Fort William College. Today it seems incredible that in Calcutta – not in Kashmir, not in Kerala, but in Calcutta, the very capital of Bengal – they could not find a teacher of Bengali. This was sufficient proof that a missionary had a much greater motivation to identify with the people of India than had either the learned Indian pundits or the British rulers. William Carey's appointment gave him an opportunity to break down the anti-missionary prejudices of the Company's top brass.

Under Grant, the Evangelical infiltration of the East India Company and the takeover of its directorate was so spectacular that historian, Ian Bradley can say, 'There was no year between 1807 and 1830 when either the Chairman or the Deputy Chairman of the Board of Directors was not an Evangelical.'

Many Indian historians don't seem to know that Lord Bentinck began to lend overt administrative support to the reforms because he too, was one of the many Evangelicals deliberately 'planted' in the higher echelons of the East India Company to 'civilize' India by transforming the Company. Bentinck was not just an Evangelical Christian but also an ardent disciple of Charles Grant. He, too, believed that the Company's first job in India could not be to make money: 'The first duty of the Imperial Government is the moral regeneration of the immense mass of our fellow creatures.'

Other Evangelicals in the leadership of the Company included famous administrators such as John Lawrence, Sir Herbert Edwards, Sir John Nicholson, and Sir Robert Montgomery. These were the men who helped build the modern Punjab as the showpiece of Colonial administration. Later, even the critics of the Evangelicals within the British Raj were grateful that the excellent work of the Christian administrators ensured that the Sikhs stayed out of the 1857 'Mutiny', guaranteeing its failure.

Today Indian historians blame the Sikhs for being traitors because they did not participate in India's 'First War of Independence'. The 'blame', in fact, belongs to those builders of modern India. Their excellent work made Sikhs then think that India's interests at that point in history were being better served by these reformer-administrators than by the feudal lords fighting for their own rule.

We can now turn to the two contributions of William Carey which are of special significance today.

First contribution – it's possible!

The primary presupposition of any reform, as we have already noticed, is that before we can improve a society, we have to admit that it is degenerate. The second pre-supposition is that a fundamental change is, in fact, pos-sible – even if the majority is against the change. (The opposition to Carey was phenomenal. It came from the British Parliament, from the Company, from the Military, from the Oriental scholars, from his own Mission Board, and also from the very people he was seeking to serve – the Indians themselves.)

Until fairly recently it used to be taken for granted, at least in theory, that reform is possible. But for two thousand years, the Hindu/Buddhist leadership in India had taught, and the masses had believed, that this earth was a place where souls were sent to take the conse-quences of their previous *karma* (deeds). Therefore, the meaning of human life, by definition, was suffering. Thus life without suffering was not possible. The only way to escape this prison of suffering was by escaping from life itself which is the Indian concept of salvation, or *nirvana*.

What, then, should a man born 'untouchable' do? Or a widow? Or a leper? The Hindu/Buddhist answer is that each has to live with their *karma* and *dharma*, as best they can, without seeking to change fate in any fundamental way.

If we add to this Hindu fatalism (produced by the doctrines of *karma*, reincarnation and *dharma*) the all-per-vasive belief that our life on earth is determined by the astrological deities above, or by the demons and demi-gods below, then we can begin to understand why schol-ars such as Sir Thomas Munro had ruled out the possibility of reform. This was not all; if *karma*, stars, and demons did leave some freedom for a person, it was severely limited by the Hindu scriptures, written, often, from Brahmanical self-interest.

We have seen that the scriptural mandates behind India's social and intellectual evils worked powerfully against reforms. Even if an individual British officer believed some Hindu customs to be wicked, he could not use the State power against those customs.

Is reform possible when religion defends evil and the State is committed not to interfere with religion? Carey's faith in a transcendent Ruler, the God of History who was above human rulers, sustained him against all odds.

One result of his success has been that since his day, most Indians (including even those who believe in *karma*, reincarnation, astrology, Brahmanical scriptures, etc.) now tend to agree that reform is possible. They are forced to reject the fatalistic idea that reform is not possible. That premise had ruled Indian civilization and ruined India for two thousand years. Carey's belief that human suffering can be and should be resisted has dominated the last two hundred years of Indian history.

Today, however, it seems certain that we cannot take it for granted that this optimistic idea will continue to be the mainstream belief. At a theoretical level Western postmodernism has already rejected the ideas of 'progress' and 'development' as mythical 'metanarratives'. The stage is set for the older Indian pessimism and fatalism to win over the earlier optimism in the twenty-first century, undoing much of what Carey and the reformers who followed him had achieved. For example, in his popular book, *The Degeneration of India*, the Chief Election Commissioner, Sheshan, argues that 'India is terminally sick.' His pessimistic diagnosis is widely believed because few people have done as much as he has to try and cleanse our public life of it's all-pervasive corruption. This growing pessimism makes it urgent for us to understand Carey's optimistic mind-set.

William Carey believed in the possibility of reform because the Bible taught that the Creator did not intend life to be suffering. God had created Adam and Eve to live in Eden – in bliss. Suffering had come later as a result of sin. Suffering is thus a historical fact, not a metaphysical truism, which means it can be and should be resisted.

Sin is not *karma*. The idea of *karma* is that an impersonal law rules our destiny and automatically gives us the consequences of our actions. According to the Bible, sin is breaking the laws of a Person – our loving heavenly Father. Therefore, it is possible, to find forgiveness and to be delivered from sin and its consequences.

It was this non-humanistic, transcendent faith which sustained Carey, and helped him to liberate India from its two-millennia-long bondage to fatalism and religious escapism.

Second contribution – language of modernization

Carey's second great contribution to the cause of India's modernization (which is currently being undermined, partly because it is inadequately understood), is his contribution to the development of India's vernacular languages.

Crucial to the European Protestant Reformers like Martin Luther was the knowledge that in order to transform his people, Christ used the language of the common man, Aramaic, rather than the Hebrew of the sacred Jewish Scriptures. Until the sixteenth century 'the languages of learning' and therefore of the élite had been Latin and Greek; whereas ordinary people in Europe spoke German, French or English. This allowed the privileged élite to exploit ignorance.

In order to liberate the masses, to make the knowledge of the truth available to all the people, the Reformers began to translate the Bible into the languages of the common people. Martin Luther himself translated the Bible into German.

Obviously, to have the Scriptures translated into the spoken language of the people is of little value if they don't read and write the language they speak. Therefore, the Reformers followed Bible translation with a drive to give a basic education to the masses. Growth of democracy and market economy in the West became possible as two of the several lasting results of their mission. It is not possible to have a government of the people, for the people, and by the people which functions mainly in the language of the élite. Nor is a genuine market economy possible without the spoken language of the people becoming also the language of learning, science, industry, and the marketplace. The genius of the market economy is that it liberates the energies of the masses for making contributions to the economic life of the country. This is impossible if an élitist language becomes a barrier, over which ordinary citizens cannot climb.

Thus, a key factor in modernization, which Carey tried to popularize is that the spoken language of the people should also be the language of learning, the language of industry, of marketing, and of governing. India has not yet taken this lesson to heart. That is one reason it has been left way behind by countries such as Japan and South Korea, whose modernization began almost a century after India's.

A feature of a medieval society is its use of an élitist language (such as Latin, Persian, Sanskrit, or now, English) as a means of discriminating, and also as a method of granting to an aristocracy unearned privileges. It became possible for India to make the transition from Persian as the court language, to Urdu, and then to the regional languages (at least, in the lower courts) because of Carey's labour and leadership in turning the vernaculars into literary languages through Bible translation.

This should help us to understand why a reformer, such as William Carey, was so obsessed with translating and/or publishing the Bible in almost 40 different languages; and why he helped start more than one hundred vernacular schools, and why he launched the first college in Asia to teach in an Asian language – Bengali. Their passion for reforming India, by making the Bible available in the vernaculars, motivated the missionaries to develop the grammar for many Indian dialects, and, eventually, to develop Hindi as a literary language for the majority of the citizens of India.

George Smith, one of William Carey's biographers, explains Carey's passion for the vernaculars thus:

> Like the growth of a tree is the development of a language...In countries like India and China, where civilization has long ago reached its highest level, and has been declining for want of the salt of a universal Christianity, it is the missionary again who interferes for the highest ends, but by a different process. Mastering the complex classical speech and literature of the learned and priestly class, and living with his Master's sympathy among the people whom that class oppresses, he takes the popular dialects which are instinct with the life of the future; where they are wildly luxuriant he brings them under law, where they are barren he enriches them from the parent stock so as to make them the vehicle of ideas such as Greek gave to Europe, and in time he brings to birth nations worthy of the name by a national language and literature lighted up with the ideas of the Book which he is the first to translate.

Today Bengali – the national language of Bangladesh – is the only Indian language which has the pride of earning a Nobel Prize for literature, for Rabindra Nath Tagore's *Gitanjali*. But we have already seen that merely ten decades before Tagore, his own city of Calcutta – the capital of Bengal – did not have one qualified teacher of Bengali. This should not be surprising, for the medieval-minded pundits considered Bengali a language, 'fit only for women and demons'. S.K.De points out in his study, *Bengali Literature in the Nineteenth Century*, that it was Carey and his missionary colleagues who,

raised the language from the debased condition of an unset-
tled dialect to the character of a regular and permanent form
of speech.

The Bengali songs of the *Gitanjali* display both the influence of the language of Carey as well as the worldview
of the Bible, which Carey translated.

It is instructive to read why Carey refused to have
English as the medium of instruction in the college he
founded at Serampore. The following is an excerpt from
the Mission Report in 1818:

> [The missionaries] apprehended that such a step, [introduc-
> tion of an English-medium education] in the first instance,
> would go towards frustrating the very design of the institu-
> tion. The moment a native youth found he had enough
> English to enable him to copy an English letter, a stop would
> have been put to his studies...They imagined there was a
> prospect of them getting Rs.16 or 20 monthly as English
> copyists in the metropolis. This course, therefore, instead of
> promoting the welfare of the country would have trans-
> formed its finest youth into mercenary copyists, ignorant of
> their own language and even of English as to any purpose
> of mental improvement.

Carey's educational efforts, very self-consciously, were
directed towards an improvement of the Indian mind, not
toward preparing an army of mercenaries for the British
Raj. Therefore, he insisted on imparting knowledge in the
language of the people, while the Company was already
teaching English to prepare its army of hirelings. The
efforts of the East India Company would never have
produced a Tagore; the missionary effort did.

An additional result of the development of Indian languages was the development of Indian nationalism. Modern nationalism had developed in Europe after the
Protestant Reformation, along with the growth of national
languages in Europe. Carey and the other missionaries
knew that a tiny British army had been able to colonize a

great country such as India, only because Hinduism had not been able to cultivate a spirit of patriotism in India. While some later missionaries were undoubtedly racists and others prostituted themselves to the Raj, overall the missionaries came to India because they loved India, and they tried to cultivate, amongst their converts, patriotism or a love for India. Their efforts began to succeed after they persuaded Michael Madhusudan Dutt – an upper-caste convert – to write his poetry in Bengali and not only in English. It was Dutt's poetry which triggered off what is often called the 'Bengali Renaissance' or the Bengali Nationalism. It produced Bankim Chandra Chatterjee, Swami Vivekananda, Rabindra Nath Tagore and finally Mahatma Gandhi.

Carey was well aware that the Indian languages were not developed enough to translate the European knowledge into them or to use them as media for higher education. Nor did they have the necessary literature. He strove therefore to develop both the vernacular languages and their literature. After a team of pundits would complete a translation of the Bible in a vernacular, he would encourage them to begin translating educational books in that same language. This work, unfortunately, was necessarily a slow process during his lifetime. Neither the Indian élite nor the East India Company provided Carey with either resources or work partners who shared his vision. The missionary societies who later, following Carey's initiative, did motivate thousands of men and women to give to India their lives and resources, at that time were just getting off the ground. Countries such as Japan and South Korea have made great advances over India, partly because they immediately translate almost every book which is worth anything.

Macaulay's Minute and 'English' education

Lord Macaulay's Minute served as a rocket booster, launching into a sustained orbit the educational revolution of India. Few Indian historians, however, seem to know that the man immediately behind Macaulay's Minute was Carey's younger contemporary, Alexander Duff, a close friend of Macaulay's brother-in law, Charles Trevelyan. Duff, who under Carey's inspiration pioneered English education in Calcutta, also started the controversy between an Oriental and an English education for India. Macaulay was asked to help resolve that controversy.

Carey had encouraged Duff to start educational institutions that imparted European education. Carey's thesis was that European education should be the substance, with the vernacular language as its medium or vehicle.

Duff agreed with Carey, but he found that the youth in Calcutta were more interested in learning English than in learning the vernacular. Besides, of course, the poverty of the Indian mind had ensured that the literature for higher education did not exist in the vernaculars. Duff, although a linguist, felt that he himself should use English as the medium for instruction, hoping that future generations of Indians would love India enough to produce the vernacular literature to help modernize thinking India. Alexander Duff wrote:

> I saw clearly and expressed myself strongly to the effect that ultimately, in a generation or two, the Bengalee, by improvement might become the fitting medium for European knowledge. But at that time it was a poor language, like English before Chaucer, and had in it, neither by translation nor original composition, no works embodying any subjects of study beyond the merest elements.

After Lord Macaulay had ruled in favour of 'English' education, Alexander Duff had the following to say about the choice between English language and the vernacular, clearly displaying Carey's influence on his thinking:

> Who, then, will hesitate in affirming that, in the *meantime*, the Government has acted wisely in appointing the English language as the medium of communicating English literature and science to the select youth of India? And who will venture to say that the wisdom of the act would be diminished if it guaranteed the continuance of English as the medium until the living spoken dialects of India became ripened, by the copious infusion of expressive terms, for the formation of a new and improved national literature?

The wisdom of Macaulay's act, unfortunately, has been diminished today. Contrary to the expectations of the pioneers of India's reform, English has simply replaced Sanskrit as the language of the learned élite. It has become the language of unfair discrimination and unearned privilege, driving India back towards medievalism.

India's medieval mind-set has misunderstood Macaulay's advocacy of an 'English' education.

To begin with, we need to know that Duff and Macaulay were not discussing the relative merits of English and the vernacular, but the relative merits of the Oriental education versus the English or European education.

The chief Orientalists, who were called the Brahmanizing Five (The Hon H.Shakespeare, H. Thoby Prinsep, James Prinsep, William Hay Macnaghten and T.C.C. Sutherland), had ensured that the Company's grant of Rs.100,000 was used for promoting the knowledge of Sanskrit, Persian, and Arabic. This was in spite of the fact that Indians themselves were uninterested in learning these languages. As Duff demonstrated in his college in Calcutta and Macaulay noted in his Minute, the students had to be paid scholarships to motivate them to study Oriental literature, while they themselves were prepared to pay for an English education. The Orientalists had been a powerful enough influence in the Company to get their proposal approved to set up a new Sanskrit College in Calcutta in 1823. This move was the last straw, resulting in a strong reaction from the enlightened Indian thinkers, such as Raja Ram Mohun Roy who denounced it as a step 'best calculated to keep this country in darkness.'

Another influential voice that opposed Oriental education was that of Bishop Heber of Calcutta, composer of the great hymn, *Holy, Holy, Holy*. He visited the Company-funded Benares Sanskrit College, and to his horror discovered that,

> Under a grant ordered by Parliament on the pressure of the Christian public (of Britain), and administered by a Christian Government, a professor lecturing on terrestrial globe, identified Mount Meroo with the North Pole, declared that the tortoise of the Hindu cosmogony supported the earth from under the South Pole, pointed to Padalon in the centre of the globe, and demonstrated how the sun went round the earth every day and visited the signs of the Zodiac!

In reaction to the above misuse of public funds for education, the 'Anglicists' such as Robert Mertins Bird, J.B. Colvin, Saunders, Bushby and Charles Trevelyan, acting under Duff's influence, argued that in India's interest the funds ought to be used for imparting a European education. They were not arguing for English language as the medium of education *per se*, but for a sharing of knowledge accumulated in England, in whatever medium was feasible. Macaulay opted for the English language as the temporary medium for what was then English or European education. He put it thus in the Minute itself:

> We ought to employ them (our funds) in teaching what is best worth knowing; that English is better worth knowing than Sanskrit or Arabic; that the natives are desirous to be taught English, and are not desirous to be taught Sanskrit or Arabic;...that it is possible to make natives of this country thoroughly good English scholars, and that to this end our efforts ought to be directed . . .

In one point I fully agree with the gentlemen to whose general views I am opposed. I feel, with them, that it is impossible for us, with our limited means, to attempt to educate the body of the people. We must do our best to form a class of persons, Indian in blood and colour, but English in taste, in opinions, in morals, and in intellect. To that class we may leave it to refine the vernacular dialects of the country, to enrich those dialects with terms of science borrowed from the Western nomenclature, and to render them, by degrees, fit vehicles for conveying knowledge to a great mass of the population.

It should be clear from the above that the long shadow of William Carey – the educationist and the great champion of the vernaculars – was cast over this Minute. It became even clearer when Macaulay was asked if it was permissible to use the same public fund to teach 'Hindee' at Ajmer. He wrote,

An order to give instruction in the English language is, by necessary implication, an order to give instruction, where that instruction is required, in the vernacular language. For what is meant by teaching a boy a foreign language? Surely this...teaching him what words in the foreign language correspond to certain words in his own vernacular language...enabling him to translate from the foreign language into his own vernacular language, and *vice versa*. We learn one language, our Mother Tongue, by noticing the correspondence between words and things. But all the languages, which we afterwards study, we learn by noticing the correspondence between the words in those languages and the words in our own Mother Tongue. The teaching the boys at Ajmer, therefore, to read and write Hindee seems to me to be *bona fide* a part of an English education.

The Reforms' grand finale

The dynamic faith of William Carey and Charles Grant in a sovereign and active God had led them to believe that

God had given India to Britain, precisely for her salvation, not for her economic exploitation as a colony. Grant wrote in his book:

> In considering the affairs of the world as under the control of the Supreme Disposer, and those distant territories...providentially put into our hands...is it not necessary to conclude that they are given to us, not merely that we might draw an annual profit from them, but that we might diffuse among their inhabitants, long sunk in darkness, vice and misery, the light and benign influence of the truth, the blessings of well-regulated society, the improvements and comforts of active industry?

Grant had therefore gone on to argue in his book that the commercial interests of England would be better served by improving India, and not by enslaving it. That this viewpoint finally won the day is illustrated when, 40 years later, in a speech in Parliament in 1833, Lord Macaulay – the son of Grant's friend Zachary Macaulay, a member of the Evangelical 'sect' of Clapham, a protégé of Wilberforce and the author of the Minute of 1835 – expounded this thesis of Grant's book. In that historic speech Macaulay argued that England must pursue this policy of improving India, even if improvement meant India's eventual independence. For, 'To trade with civilized men is infinitely more profitable than to govern savages.' The following is a sample of the power of Macaulay's language and logic that overwhelmed the Parliament:

> It may be that the public mind of India may expand under our system till it has outgrown that system; that by good government we may educate our subjects into a capacity for better government, that having become interested in European knowledge, they may in some future age, demand European institutions (of freedom). Whether such a day will ever come I know not. But never will I attempt to avert or retard it. Whenever it comes it will be the proudest day in English history. To have found a great people sunk in the

lowest depths of slavery and superstitions, to have so ruled them as to have made them desirous and capable of all the privileges of citizens, would indeed be a title to glory all our own. The sceptre may pass away from us. Unforeseen accidents may derange our most profound schemes of policy. Victory may be inconstant to our arms. But there are triumphs which are followed by no reverse. There is an empire exempt from all natural causes of decay. Those triumphs are the pacific triumphs of reason over barbarism; that empire is the imperishable empire of our arts and our morals, our literature and our laws.

The radical difference a spiritual conversion made in these Evangelical reformers is exemplified by their understanding of what the British conquest of India should mean. It is the very opposite of the typical British attitudes mentioned at the beginning of this chapter.

Charles Trevelyan, Macaulay's brother-in-law, summed up the long-term aim of the Christian Reform Movement, in 1838 in his pamphlet on *Education In India*. (Needless to say, Macaulay and Trevelyan were articulating what Carey had already practiced and demonstrated.) Trevelyan wrote:

The existing connexion between two such distant countries as England and India, cannot, in the nature of things, be permanent: no effort of policy can prevent the natives from ultimately regaining their independence. But there are two ways of arriving at this point. One of these is through the medium of revolution; the other through that of reform...(Revolution) must end in the complete alienation of mind and separation of interests between ourselves and the natives; the other (reform) in a permanent alliance, founded on mutual benefit and good-will. The only means at our disposal for preventing (revolution) and securing...the results (of reform) is, to set the natives on a process of European improvement...the natives will have independence, after first learning how to make good use of it; and we shall exchange profitable subjects for still more profitable allies...Trained by us to happiness and independence, and endowed with our learning and political institutions, India will remain the proudest monument of British benevolence...

That anticipated day of India's Independence and (Evangelical) England's ultimate triumph finally came in 1947. Macaulay had anticipated it almost prophetically more than a century earlier. India asked for and became independent of the British Raj. Yet it retained and resolved to live by the British laws and institutions, as a member of the British Commonwealth. For example, the Indian Penal Code of 1861 which is still the basis for law in Indian jurisprudence, was drafted by Macaulay himself as 'Codes of Criminal and Civil Procedures', when he served as India's Law Minister.

Thus India's Independence in 1947 was not only a victory for Mahatma Gandhi and the 'Freedom Fighters', but even more fundamentally, a triumph for Carey's Evangelical England. It marked the victory of the early missionaries over the narrow commercial, political, and military vested interests of England, as well as a victory for the heart and mind of India.

The violent movements and the human rights violations of the 1970s, '80s and early '90s raise serious doubts about whether or not human rights and freedoms will last for long in India. They cannot last if we choose to forget the faith and spirit of India's modernizers.

5

The Mind of a Modernizer

The question

Why would William Carey oppose *sati*, when he had himself observed that it was the widow's 'voluntary choice' to be immolated on her husband's funeral pyre? Did he not believe in the right of the individual to make a free choice?

Or, how could he assume that his efforts would help change a centuries' old religious-cultural tradition in Hindu India, administered by an irreligious British company which would not even permit a British missionary to reside in its territory?

This chapter is concerned with the question: *Why did Carey attempt what he did?* Why couldn't Indians or other British leaders initiate what he ventured to do? And, for that matter, why don't Indian Christians today walk in his footsteps, in this area of reform?

The central thesis of this chapter is that certain conscious or unconscious theological assumptions served as one of the basic dynamics behind William Carey's work. A knowledge of these truths came from his understanding of the Bible. Many segments of the Christian church today have ignored these basics of their doctrinal heritage. That is ironic, because even the Hindu reformers of the nineteenth century had accepted at least some of these beliefs, as being essential for their task of modernizing India.

Without recovering these basics, we will succeed merely in a hollow 'celebration' of the Bicentenary of Carey's arrival in India. We could, no doubt, feel a second-hand or vicarious glory from his achievements, but if Carey is to become more than a 'hero' – a model who inspires radical discipleship – then it is imperative that his theological assumptions are understood and that they are taught from our pulpits.

The social climate of his day, and the historical factors that forged his mentality and his priorities were, obviously, significant. Nevertheless, his background and environment elicited a particular response from Carey because of his prior theological assumptions. While we cannot recreate history, there is nothing to prevent us from recovering the dynamics of his theological assumptions – the mind of a modernizer.

The following aspects of Carey's world view seem to me to be most relevant for reform and modernization.. Most people never articulate the world view which forms the intellectual grid through which they understand and respond to their environment. Therefore, it is not necessary to assume that Carey was always conscious of his theological reasons for reacting the way he did.

God as the Creator: the doctrine of Creation and Science

Carey's deep and dogged interest in nature – in stones (Geology), in insects (Biology), in plants and flowers (Botany and Agriculture), in trees (Forestry), and in the stars (Astronomy) – was rooted in his understanding that this world was his Father's creation.

Obviously, the intellectual climate of England in which William Carey grew up was important in shaping his interest in studying natural science, in publishing scientific books, and in teaching science to his students. This scientific climate in England was a result of the biblical teaching that God had created the cosmos with his *Logos*. The *Logos* is translated as 'Word', 'Wisdom', or 'Reason'. The Bible taught that human beings were created with minds similar to God's own rationality, so that we may understand the laws of nature and manage the earth. Thus, Carey was interested in the physical universe around him because he believed that our heavenly Father had blessed mankind, both with a rationality to understand the creation and with an authority to govern it.

Creation and the inductive method of knowledge

The doctrine of Creation as taught in Genesis 1 had already given birth to the inductive method of knowledge before Carey. Theological assumptions, that (a) the universe is a stable system run by rational laws ordained by God, and (b) that the universe is a book of God's 'natural revelation' which can be and ought to be read by us, so that we may both (c) learn about God's wisdom and power and also (d) govern the earth, implied that *objective knowledge was possible through careful observation*.

Carey's *Enquiry* reflects a mind that investigated the facts. His entire appeal for world mission was based on meticulously collected data, not on an appeal of emotions of the moment. One can say that the inductive method which John Calvin had applied to the Scriptures in his *Institutes*, and which served as the foundation for the Scientific Method articulated by Francis Bacon was, for the first time, applied by Carey to the field of Missiology. The same methodology – finding objective facts (say, about *sati*, with the help of researchers) – made Carey's writings so powerful.

It should be obvious that this 'religious' theory of how

knowledge of truth (Epistemology) was to be obtained, was the exact opposite of mystical, magical, and esoteric ideas of knowledge then prevalent in India. Hindus did not translate their scriptures from Sanskrit into the languages of the people because truth was not something to be understood rationally. It was to be experienced by 'killing' the intellect through various means of meditation and yoga. In some religious traditions such as Tantra, a deliberately ambiguous and misleading language called *sandha-bhasha* was used, both to confuse and discourage the non-initiate and also to remind the enlightened tantric that the reality he sought was beyond logical rationality. Even the non-tantric religions sought to annihilate meaningful/rational language through *mantras.* A mantra is a systematic annihilation of meaningful language by mechanical repetition of a word or sound. In Hinduism, destruction of rationality was presumed to be a precondition for obtaining a knowledge of truth. Science, based on observation or inductive method, was thus ruled out *a priori*, by India's religious tradition.

Philosophies that undermine science

The lack today of a similar interest in the natural sciences in the Indian Church is rooted in a spirituality which sees God as Saviour, but fails to appreciate him as the Creator. Some versions of a new spiritual trend among Christians, known as spiritual warfare, also accept, perhaps unconsciously, the essence of polytheism. They refuse to see that much of the occult phenomenon is hoax, not genuine instances of demons and demigods influencing material reality. In reacting to a secularized-materialistic science, they undermine a basic feature of the biblical world view, which is that the material realm is normally a stable order, open to scientific investigation, except when there is a miracle – an unusual supernatural intervention.[1]

The Hindu mind-set at Carey's time did not acknowledge God as the Creator. Creation was considered to be either a dream of God (*maya* or illusion), or worse still, creation itself was deified as divinity.

An implication of viewing creation as *maya* or illusion, is to dislike it – to seek isolation or escape from it, not to love it and care for it.

The result of seeing the Creator and creation as one is to fall into the bondage of idolatry or mysticism. If creation is divine then we can fear it, worship it, absolutize it, or seek to become one with it, but we cannot assume the responsibility of understanding, managing, or changing it.

William Carey found India in the grip of chronic deprivation because while in *folk Hinduism* idolatry and polytheism, i.e. the worship of creation and gods and goddesses, had rendered the human mind incapable of governing creation and harnessing its potential for development, in *philosophic Hinduism* mysticism had undercut the motivational and epistemological foundations of science.

Science and technology are a result of human desire to enjoy nature by understanding it, subduing it, and by establishing our rule over it. Science is based on the assumption that the universe is a stable-rational order. Polytheism and the occult, on the other hand, demolish the possibility of science by assuming that the natural universe is an unstable magical system constantly changing according to the whims and fancies of supernatural

---

[1] The concept of 'spiritual warfare' in its most damaging manifestation in the Indian context is unbiblical in denying the sovereignty of God. It suggests that territorial spirits, not God, rule, reinforcing Hindu polytheism and New Age spiritism. Man was created to have domination over the planet and he has to assume responsibility for what goes wrong: passing the buck onto spirit entities further undermines the significance of human choices, already problematic in India.

beings. Mysticism can motivate us only to enjoy nature by feeling it in a non-rational way. Science has to be able to trust human rationality as a valid source of knowledge. Mysticism requires a systematic obliteration of rationality. Science has to insist on objectivity, even while recognizing that we are subjects trying to be objective. Mysticism also precludes science because it begins when we cease being objective in our observation.

Creation and ecology

Today, there is a naive and mistaken notion in the West that our environmental crisis is a result of the human desire to have dominion over creation. The fact, on the contrary, is that we cannot manage the environment unless we see ourselves both as an integral *part of* creation, therefore dependent on it, but also *over* creation, therefore responsible for it. The environmental mess in India, which is far worse than in the industrialized West, is a clear indication that the worship of nature damages creation more than do our attempts to manage it. It is enough here to point out that it was William Carey and not the Hindu mystics who initiated the struggle for regenerating the eco-balance in India.

Creation and social reform

An implication of the belief that God is the Creator is that he is transcendent – apart from the physical and social realms, and above them. Our ability to change our physical, social or political environment, as we shall see, is directly proportional to our ability to grasp both the significance of God's transcendence and authority over creation and also our God-given authority over creation.

A second ramification of the belief that God is the Creator also served as a decisive determinant in the modernization of India. In this basic tenet Carey found a moral basis for opposing evils such as *sati*. Many Indian reformers (e.g. Jotiba Phule) who succeeded Carey found this idea compelling. Today, ironically, the Western world, in a self-destructive mood, seems to be turning away from the implication that, *if God is the author of a universe that exits objectively, (independent from our experience of it) then reality – whether natural, social or moral – has a given meaning and definition. This meaning is independent from how we perceive the universe around us.*

The significance of this principle for reform can be illustrated with Carey's battle against *sati*.

An illustration

The culture of idol-worship assumes that we are free to decide if a stone is a god or not. It implies that God has not given a revelation of the objective truth to mankind, therefore we can define reality ourselves and give to it whatever meaning we prefer. If this assumption is true, then a woman is free to imagine that her husband is her god; and that she lives for him. Therefore, after he dies her own life has no meaning. This outrageous conclusion served as the hidden basis for a justification of *sati*.

For Carey, however, ultimately it was God who, as the Creator, gave meaning and definition to his creation. God decides who we are, and what the true nature of the husband/wife relationship is, or what it ought to be. Therefore, neither one's society, nor an individual, is finally free to define himself and/or his relationships.

This belief meant that Carey had no problem in judging whether or not *sati* was evil. For him the relevant question was not whether or not *sati* was a voluntary act of a woman, or whether she was forced to kill herself. The objective fact, as far as Carey was concerned, was that a woman's life was neither her own, nor her husband's. It was God's. And the Creator had not given to us the right to violate his gift of life. Suicide is sin because it considers a life valueless which is, in fact, precious to the Creator; it sees a situation to be hopeless where God expects faith and patience.

Contemporary relevance

This theological factor is of enormous significance in the current Indian debate on *sati*, which started with the Roop Kanwar episode[2] in September 1987. The matter is still *sub-judice*. Depending on how the court views the case, it could revive the hideous tradition of widow-burning.[3]

The following two factors make the danger of *sati*'s revival a real possibility:

First, the democratic temper of our times suggests to many people that in the ultimate sense, the majority decides what is right or what is wrong. So, if the majority favours *sati*, it ought to be permitted.

The *second* factor is the current ('New Age') belief that an individual is totally free to define his or her own reality. We indeed have freedom, but our freedom is limited because our freedom comes, not from being God, but from

---

[2] Roop Kanwar, an 18-year-old upper-caste widow, committed *sati* in 1987 in a village in Rajasthan. The national press in India reported it as a three-line news item on a back page. Thirteen days later I followed up with a front page piece for the *Indian Express* – and it became a major national controversy. Such coverage has put Hindu women's rights on the national agenda for the first time since the Independence in 1947.

[3.] At the end of 1996 the court acquitted Roop Kanwar's relatives charged with abetting *Sati*. The press has been filled with stories of how *Sati* is currently being glorified in the state of Rajasthan - millions throng the temples dedicated to women who committed *Sati*. Their picture postcards are used as greeting cards, etc.

the fact (as we will consider later) that we are made in the image of God. We are not programmed machines, but persons with freedom of choice. We are therefore at liberty to have subjective/private perceptions of reality. This, too, has important implications for the process of modernization: it sets us free to be creative. However, since God is the Creator of the universe, including ourselves, reality already has an objective meaning given to it by him. God's revelation sets limits to our freedom. We sin when we cross those limits. For example, a woman is free to see her husband as a lover, or as an oppressor; as her master, or as her partner, or consider herself as his slave. But she is not free to see him as her God. That, the Creator says, is idolatry and therefore, sin.

It is possible to imagine that a group of Hindus could decide that a revival of *sati* would be a symbolic necessity for ridding India of its cultural colonization by 'Christian England'. If a group decided to force a nation-wide showdown on the issue (whether or not a Hindu woman is free to abide by her conscience to commit *sati*) then I have no doubt that the pro-*sati* lobby would win in India (just as the pro-abortion and pro-euthanasia lobbies have, for now, won in the West). I think the pro-*sati* lobby would win because the so-called 'democratic' temper of our times and the modern idea of unbounded individual freedom favour their viewpoint.

The practice of *sati* does meet certain social needs, just as abortion, infanticide and euthanasia do: the death of a high-caste man creates some peculiar socio-economic problems and by eliminating the widow, *sati* eliminates those problems. For example, if a widow remarries, does she take her husband's family property into another family or into another caste? If she could, then the poorer, lower caste young men would love to marry the higher caste widows!

The pro-*sati* lobby was defeated in the Privy-Council

in London in the early 1830s, only because the British mind then shared Carey's theological assumption that the final source of Law is the Law-giver, the Creator, not an individual, nor the consensus of a society. We would have lived like amoral animals if the Creator had not made us in his image, i.e., with the ability to make value judgements – both aesthetic and moral. In this sense, the Law is what the Creator describes as the moral reality. Neither an individual, nor the majority is free to violate the divinely-ordained moral categories.

(We may note that even though Ram Mohun Roy's defence of the edict before the Privy-Council was helpful and received well-deserved media attention, it was not as significant a factor as the Indian historians make it out to be. The Council members included at least two close friends of Carey. One of them, Lord Wellesley, as already mentioned, had been convinced by Carey that *sati* was evil as early as 1806, 25 years before Ram Mohun Roy argued the same case before the Council in London.)

Needless to say, the prejudices of India's present judicial and political leaders at this point could be as decisive as the pressure of liberal public opinion. If the judiciary were to acquit Roop Kanwar's family on the grounds that there was no evidence that they had forced her to commit *sati*, then it would encourage other families to follow her example. Indian politicians today are bound to feel that the pro-*sati*, high-caste 'vote bank' is more important than what Carey or Lord Bentinck thought two centuries ago.

Our generation is guided more by how we 'feel about an issue', than by the facts of the situation. But, am I to take care of the creation because of how I feel about a particular issue or a species? Or am I to take care of it because I was created for that purpose? For the sake of the future of human civilization it is immensely important to recover, in our day, the truth that an objective physical and moral universe exists (independently of our perception);

that God is its Author; that he, ultimately, defines it and gives value and meaning to it; and that we have to abide by his word irrespective of how we feel.

Human beings as God's image

A modernizer has simultaneously to hold on to two elementary beliefs: *first*, that a given physical-moral reality exits independently of their perception, and *second*, that they can alter what exists according to their imagination.

That may sound obvious today. When Carey arrived in India, he found a civilization that had deliberately denied both those essential beliefs and consequently was powerless to improve.

Both these ideas formed part of the mind-set of William Carey. On the one hand the Bible affirmed that the objective universe had a definition and meaning given by the Creator himself. Yet, on the other hand, the same Bible also liberated post-Reformation Europe to imagine and create a world better than that which they experienced. This freedom to be imaginative and creative was fundamental to the reforms and developments of the centuries immediately preceding Carey.

Let us first mention an obvious implication of the doctrine that human beings are made in God's image, after which we can look at other implications which are not so obvious in our day.

Human life is precious

It should not require much imagination to see that Carey's struggle to save the lives of innocent infants – the potential victims of infanticide; widows – the potential victims of *sati*; and lepers – the potential victims of our cultural beastliness, was rooted in his understanding that human life is precious because men and women are neither machines, nor animals, but persons created in God's image. The Bible prohibited murder precisely on this premise.

What, perhaps, does need to be mentioned is that many Christians today fail to standup in defence of human life, because they think that the human soul alone reflects God's image.

By *imago Dei*, or the 'image of God', the Bible, of course, does not mean that God has a physical form such as our own. What it does mean is that when God breathed into Adam, and he became a 'living soul' – a unity of body and spirit he began to share, in a finite way, some of God's attributes such as: self-awareness, rational intelligence, volition, verbal communication, creativity, ability to make value judgements and to rule, i.e., to impose on the external environment the results of his intellect, will, and verdicts. A human being, even though a sinner, is precious because he is the crown of God's creativity on this earth.

The Hindu mind which Carey encountered had no such philosophic basis for fighting, either to preserve human life or to affirm its dignity. On the contrary, it pictured human life as being in bondage to the wheel of '*samsara*'. Individuality, according to Hinduism was, at best, suffering, and at worst a hideous illusion. Almost the entire mainstream Indian orientation had been a negation of life. When it did affirm life, such as in the Tantric tradition, it tended to exalt the sordid. The process of modernization had to begin with someone who was committed to the biblical view that even the life of a leper or a cobbler is precious, and that every human being has to be transformed until he or she fully reflects God's glory.

We share something of God's transcendence over nature

The Oxford English Dictionary defines God's transcendence as 'existing apart from, not subject to limitations of, the material universe'. A disembodied spirit exists apart from and without some of the limitations of physical laws such as gravity.

Our physical bodies are a part of the material universe and subject to its limitations. ('Dust thou art, and to dust thou shall return.') But being made in God's image means that even as physical beings, we can transcend some of the limitations of nature and alter physical reality. For example, in a dark room animals have to resign themselves to darkness, but we don't need to. Similarly, in a desert we can bring water. We are not completely limited by external reality. God has made us creative. We are free to imagine a different and better physical, social, and political world. Where there is oppression, we can dream freedom and dignity for the smallest individual.

Transcending Reality In our Imagination And Arts.

Carey is a classic example of Christian thinking not ruled by fatalistic resignation. Instead, we should use our creative imagination to make a difference. Being made in God's image has ramifications both for scientific innovations and for social reform. God saw physical darkness and, as we read in Genesis, he proceeded to create light. Later, in the gospels we read that he saw our moral-social darkness and sent Jesus to be the 'Light of Life.' As God's children, we too have to transcend the natural/social scene around us and make a difference. Jesus said to his disciples, 'You are the light of the world.'

William Carey was not surprised by the moral and social darkness that he saw in India, nor did he accept it as final or unchangeable. He knew that he had been sent to India to be light, and he sought to make a difference to his surroundings.

It cannot be denied that today the Indian mood, including the mood of Indian Christians, is pessimistic. Many think that the social evils of caste and political corruption in India are the given facts of life – beyond transformation. This mentality results from a lack of understanding that we are created qualitatively different so that we can make a difference in our environment.

Creativity and imagination are often expressed first of all in arts and literature. For example, Europe experienced the darkness of the holocaust in the 1940s, and it produced powerful works of art about that dark period. Those literary and artistic works have had such a profound impact on the present generation that it is difficult to imagine similar, state-sponsored brutalities ever being repeated there. During the partition of India and Pakistan in 1947 the Indian Subcontinent went through its own version of a 'holocaust' – a massacre of Hindus, Sikhs and Muslims by each other. Yet no comparable works of imagination and creativity were created to lament and counter that darkness. The result is that even today, the Indian mind is not ashamed of communal killings. They have become a regular feature of social life, blatantly encouraged by 'religious' and political leaders! Indians have resigned themselves to live with the darkness of communal clashes.

William Carey used his imagination in the literary arena to make a difference in his social environment. Carey wrote his *Colloquies* - 'a lively depiction of manners and notions of the people of Bengal' – as a contribution to Bengali literature. He encouraged and published both comical and literary books such as *Tota Itihas* – 'Parrot's History'!

Where Carey saw barren wilderness, he did not revert to lamenting, but began to plan forests. He studied trees, planted them, and then taught forestry. Where he saw weeds, he imagined gardens, cultivated them, published books and established forums such as the Agri-Horticultural Society of India to help give sustained support to his initiatives.

Undoubtedly the spiritual bankruptcy of many Christians in our time is closely related to the bankruptcy of godly imagination. True, many Christians do seek to be transformed into the moral image of God, but there is little desire among Indian Christians to exercise the creative dimension in them of the Maker's image. Many church leaders and their congregations in India do not plan worship services creatively, let alone plan for the landscaping of their church compounds or for the surrounding countryside. (Needless to say, many of the Hindu pilgrim centers, in spite of being wealthier than churches, are aesthetically even worse. They offer a study in contrast between God-made beauty and religion- inspired ugliness.)

Transcending reality through work

In Carey's mind imagination itself was not reality. Today, in some circles of 'alternative therapy' the practice of 'creative visualization' has become very popular. Some of our physical illnesses that are rooted in our own choices and feelings can indeed be cured by this practice because mind does transcend matter. However, it is foolishness to think that all reality is in the mind, and to look upon meditation as a panacea for our ecological and other external problems.

Carey knew that the cosmos is a result, not only of God's thought, but also of his work. We too are created to work hard to establish our rule on earth. Carey was not simply an imaginative person; he saw himself primarily as a worker. And for him, 'work' was not merely a job or a career, but a means of establishing human 'dominion' over the material realm . . . a means of partially realizing God's image in ourselves.

The Evangelicals of Carey's generation were convinced that we become less of God's image when we choose to be lazy. Many of them religiously wrote their daily journals and, if they thought that they had wasted time on a particular day, they repented. Wasting time, not being diligent in work, were serious moral issues for them. This attitude, a key factor behind the modernization of Europe, has been called the 'Protestant work ethic'. It helped Protestant Europe to march ahead of non-Protestant Europe.

Carey injected this work ethic into Indian society. The Hindu spirituality had taken the best of India's children away from work, into *ashrams* – which etymologically means *a*(non)-*shram*(labour). To be spiritual in India implied the very opposite of what Carey understood it to mean: in India to be spiritual meant to meditate, not labour. When the Divinity is seen as an impersonal consciousness or energy, and man is assumed to be divine, then spirituality is automatically an attempt to depersonalize ourselves. Hindu religious discipline, therefore, was an attempt to annihilate human rationality through mysticism, language through *mantra*, creative imagination through *yoga* or systematic emptying of the mind, and work through meditation and the *ashram* system. In this milieu Carey's religious ethic of work was a revolution.

We are meant to have dominion over time

Should our times be governed by our 'stars', via astrologers, or are we created to plan and manage our time? In other words, are we created in the image of our stars, or in the image of God who created the 'stars' and rules over them? These are not theoretical issues. A society's answers to them substantially determines whether it will advance, or remain static and under-developed.

By introducing a study of Astronomy in the classroom,

Carey brought the modernizing idea that space and time were a part of the physical world we were made to govern. The Hindu ideas of four *Yugas* (periods in a cosmic cycle) and reincarnation, as well as the all-pervasive faith in astrology, had conspired to relegate individuality to a transient phenomenon in time. If our times are ruled by our stars, then we cannot plan or manage our days and hours in terms of our own goals. We have to wait for the set 'auspicious moments'.

Carey's interest in Astronomy came from the fact that with the help of the stars, sailors such as Captain Cook had opened the sea routes for European trade with the Far East. Carey felt that Christians ought to use these routes for missions. But there was also a more basic theological dimension to his interest in astronomy.

Various means of divination, including astrology, had enslaved the human spirit in India with chains of fear and superstition, making it vulnerable to exploitation by unscrupulous priests and astrologers. This made biblical injunctions against divination come alive in Carey's mind, reassuring him that God's word was the light that India needed for her emancipation.

The Bible teaches (in Genesis 1:14–18) that the sun and the moon are not deities, but objects created to govern the day and the night. Along with the other heavenly bodies, they were created also as 'signs', or 'markers', for giving us a sense of direction, as well as a feel for history – for days and years and seasons. This means that human beings who are created to 'subdue the earth and have dominion over it' could study Geography and History because of the reference points provided by these heavenly bodies and thus 'govern'. Putting it differently: if the heavenly bodies were not there, or were invisible, we could not know North from South, or day from night, let alone make calendars.

The sun and the moon, as markers, the Bible says,

divide time for us into small and manageable parts so that we can plan our work and obey the command to work for six days and rest on the seventh. Without markers by which to divide our time, we would invariably carry over one week's work into the next. We would not be able to plan, or to manage, or to govern.

India's backwardness is substantially rooted in the false view of time propagated by her religious teachers. Development requires a correct understanding of human destiny in relation to the universe of space and time.

Human beings are above time, *firstly*, by virtue of the fact that we share God's image who is above the universe of space and time, and *secondly*, because we were made to live 'forever'. Our individuality is not a passing phenomenon which will be reincarnated as something else the next time round. Adam, as Adam, was created to live forever. That changed after sin entered the scene. One of sin's consequences was death. Death has put human beings 'under time'; we die, while time appears to go on and on.

Carey had come to preach the Good News of Jesus Christ, which says that human beings can once again have 'eternal life'. When Jesus died on the cross, he took our sin and its result – death – upon himself. When he rose again from the dead, he defeated death – our final enemy.The New Testament teaches that Christ's resurrection has colossal consequences for us.

The resurrected Jesus said, 'I am the beginning and the end.' If we are in him, we will also reign with him for ever. 'For ever' means that we are not under time, but above it. While, as created beings we will always remain finite, we can still have the authority to plan and manage the course of our days and years, just as we can also regulate the course of a river, or order the crops of a field.

In resisting the 'superstitions' of Indian culture, such as faith in astrology, palmistry and other forms of divination, and by the teaching of the resurrection – God's triumph over death in history – Carey was setting India free from an enslaving concept of time; he was modernizing the Indian mind at a very fundamental level.

We share God's transcendence over 'powers and principalities'

For Carey's contemporaries, one of the biggest deterrents to mission were the oppressive socio-political power structures of the 'heathen' countries such as India. Having grown up in 'civilized' societies, they could not consider living in countries governed by the 'laws of the jungle'. Carey confronted this objection head-on in his *Enquiry*:

> As to their uncivilized, and barbarous way of living, this can be no objection (to mission)...It was no objection to the apostles and their successors, who went among the barbarous Germans and Gauls, and still more barbarous Britons! They did not wait for the ancient inhabitants of these countries to be civilized before they could be Christianized, but went simply with the doctrine of the Cross; and Tertullian could boast that 'those parts of Britain which were proof against the Roman armies, were conquered by the Gospel of Christ' – it was no objection to an Elliot, or a Brainerd, in later times. They went forth, and encountered every difficulty of the kind, and found that a cordial reception of the Gospel produced those happy effects which the longest intercourse with Europeans, without it, could never accomplish...After all, the uncivilized state of the heathen, instead of affording an objection *against* preaching the Gospel to them, ought to furnish an argument *for* it...Can we hear that they are without the Gospel, without government, without laws, and without arts, and sciences, and not exert ourselves to introduce amongst them the sentiments of men, and of Christians? Would not the spread of the Gospel be the most effectual means of their civilization? Would not that make them useful members of society?

Likewise, Carey begins the introduction of the *Enquiry* with these words:

> As our blessed Lord has required us to pray that His kingdom may come, and His will be done on earth as it is in heaven, it becomes us not only to express our desires of that event by words, but to use every lawful method to spread the knowledge of His name...Sin was introduced amongst the children of men by the fall of Adam, and has ever since been spreading...Yet God repeatedly made known His intention to prevail finally over all the power of the Devil, and to destroy all his works, and set up His own kingdom and interest among men, and extend it as universally as Satan had extended his. It was for this purpose that the Messiah came and died, that God might be just and the justifier of all that should believe in Him. When He had laid down His life, and taken it up again, He sent forth his disciples to preach the good tidings to every creature, and to endeavour by all possible methods to bring over a lost world to God.

What made Carey so confident that the oppressive social and political structures of this world can be reformed? One cause was the obvious cultural impact of the Wesleyan revivals, already becoming apparent in his own generation. But a more important reason was his understanding that the Lord himself had promised that darkness would not overcome the light, and that the Gospel was like the small amount of leaven, put into a batch of flour, that gradually transformed the whole dough.

It should be clear from the above quotations that Carey was a modernizer chiefly because his mind was motivated by a theological optimism: Satan's kingdom had already been defeated in history, by the death and resurrection of Jesus; Christ was already King over all the kings of this world; believers were already seated with Christ who, in turn, was above all powers and principalities of this dark age. Therefore, Carey understood that Christ's command to, 'Make disciples of every nation, teaching them to observe all My teachings', implied that the nations could be discipled before Christ's return.

The tragedy of our times is that while many Christians have confidence in the power of the Lord to return and change the world, many of us do not have confidence in the power of the Gospel to transform society now. Carey struggled against specific social evils, just as his friends in England were continuing their struggle against evils. But Carey's confidence was not in his social protest or social action, but in the Gospel. This is the very opposite of those Christians who put their hope for change in their 'social action'. It is also different from the faith of those who believe that the world can improve only after the Lord Jesus Christ will return. Carey became a reformer because he understood the breadth of the theological concept of the 'Kingdom of God'. He believed that if we disciple nations, we will increasingly see God's will being done here on earth.

Lord Wellesley and William Carey were deeply aware of the immorality among the young men, aged fifteen to twenty years, who were arriving from England to administer India. Carey believed that he could influence the political administration of India, since Jesus Christ was above the powers and principalities of the world, and Carey himself was his servant. Therefore, besides teaching languages to the newly arrived administrators, Carey strove for three decades to shape their moral character as well. As a missionary, his priorities were naturally opposite to those of the Company's servants, who had come to India to create wealth for themselves and for their nation. His compassion for the needs of India together with his gentleness were a great influence on his British pupils.[1]

[1.] Both Fort William College in Calcutta, and Hailebury College in England, where the civil servants were trained to administer India, were run by Evangelical missionaries and clergy.

Even the most skeptical of the Indian historians have to admit that, during Carey's tenure as a teacher, the character of the civil servant trainees underwent a radical transformation.

India became a showpiece of colonial administration – that is, it was better governed than the colonies of Germany, France, Holland and Denmark. There can be no doubt that the continuing decline in the moral and professional standards in the Indian Civil Service is an indication of the deliberate rejection of Carey's heritage.

Our call, however, is not to succumb to resignation and mourning for what is lost. We are called to summon the nation to repentance and to suffer for righteousness. The nation has lost its standards because the church has forgotten the truth that it is seated with Christ above all powers and principalities of this dark age. It is sad that those Christians who talk the most about the 'spiritual warfare' against the powers and principalities, seem to understand it the least. Today they tend to see themselves primarily as a 'minority besieged by satanic powers and principalities'. They don't seem to realize that they are servants of the One who claimed, 'All power is given unto me in heaven and on the earth'. Some Christians are so paralysed by a minority-complex that they keep casting demons from, say, the broken-down refrigerators but they never, lamentably, become a reforming force.

All people can change because we are all made in God's image

For Carey another implication of the fact that we are made in God's image was that even the most wretched of this world, 'the scum of the earth', can be transformed. Carey was well aware of the depravity in the countries where he wanted to see missions become active. Yet, he wrote in his *Enquiry*:

Barbarous as these poor heathens are, they appear to be as capable of knowledge as we are; and in many places, at least, have discovered uncommon genius and tractableness ...

Carey, himself, had humble origins. As a shoemaker in England, he had found that God's grace was sufficient for him. He rejected the British class system and actively opposed the racism inherent in the slavetrade, refusing to buy goods made by slave labour. It follows that it was not possible for him to condone the caste system in India.

At the outset Carey understood that his open social intercourse with Untouchables would, at least initially, slow the rate of conversions. Yet he chose not to compromise with caste distinctions – a fundamental evil of Indian society. His mission was not to collect a large number of 'converts' but to see God's overall will being done in individual lives and in the culture of India.

Carey knew that ultimately, his commitment to truth alone would be fruitful. After a low-caste person was baptized, he would celebrate by sitting and eating with the converts from all castes and with Europeans, the colonial rulers – a revolutionary gesture at that time. Until today, sadly, such behaviour is radical in India's caste-ridden society.

Virtually from every part of India we still hear stories of Christian leaders refusing to accept low-caste people into church membership because they allegedly, 'lower the cultural, intellectual, and even moral standing of the church'.

This attitude, among other factors, is undoubtedly a result of a lack of confidence in the power of the Gospel to restore God's image to the lowly. Carey remained committed to the downtrodden till the end of his life because he believed that every human being could choose to become a child of God.

God calls individuals

Initially, Fort William College refused to appoint Carey as a full professor because he was not an Anglican. Instead he was offered a tutorship earning only Rs.500 instead of Rs.1,500. For most of us, today, it is incomprehensible that out of this salary Carey would keep only Rs.40 as pocket money for himself, and give the balance to his Mission.

Obviously, to understand Carey, we need to understand Carey's view of vocation, an important concept of Protestant Christianity during his time.

Vocation and work

The idea of vocation is illustrated by a New Testament missionary, St Paul. When Paul had his conversion experience on the road to Damascus, he was 'called' to be an apostle to the Gentiles. It was an honour to be called personally by the Lord of the Universe to do something special for him. Therefore, Paul – a thinker and a teacher – was willing to stitch tents, on occasion, so that he might have the economic resources to fulfil his 'calling' or vocation.

William Perkins (1558-1602), a Puritan theologian, in his *Treatise On Calling*, (published more than a century before Carey), taught that as soon as a person becomes a Christian, they should be taught to wait upon the Lord, to find out from the Lord what their calling is. Today we do teach about prayer, Bible study, evangelism, and social work, but not about that most personal meeting with God. At best, our 'work' is understood as our 'vocation'. Our work can also be our vocation, but it is not always so. Carey's calling was not to work in an indigo factory, but he was prepared to take up such work for the sake of his vocation.

Unlike Carey, our young people will continue to seek the best paid, most secure and the least demanding jobs as long as work is understood in secular terms— as a job (making money), or a career (pursuing power, prestige and influence)—and work is automatically baptized 'vocation'. Truly, however, a missionary is a 'called one' who waits on the Lord to be commissioned by him. A missionary is thus a reformer because they a person of destiny.

Vocation and destiny

Hinduism could not produce a man such as Carey because the idea of individual destiny is alien to Hindu culture which emphasizes the dissolution of one's individuality, not its fulfilment. In fact, most people who speak Hindi, my mother-tongue, would not even know that a Hindi equivalent for the word 'destiny' exists in dictionaries. (I have never read or heard the word, only seen it in the dictionary.) The word commonly used, and the idea that dominates Hindi literature is 'fate' – the exact opposite of what the Christian concept of destiny means.

It is a serious matter that the Western cinema, for example, seems more interested today in glamorizing the very ideas that had destroyed Indian civilization – the concepts of *karma* and fate. If one were to judge the contemporary Western civilization by its entertainment media it would seem that the notion of destiny – the force which propelled men such as William Carey to heroic and altruistic service – has now been lost.

The industry and staying power of a William Carey cannot be recovered by the Indian Church unless our pulpits recover the lost doctrine of Vocation, i.e. unless we experience the reality that God wants to enter into a personal and direct working partnership with individuals who have become his children. Everyone wants a nine-to-five job. Carey had a five-to-ten job (i.e. 5.00 a.m. to 10.00 or 11.00 p.m.). He persevered because he was assigned a mission by God himself.

Vocation and individualism

Carey's heroism – a result of his understanding of vocation and destiny – represents the best form of Western individualism which followed the Protestant Reformation. One central emphasis of the Gospel is that each individual has to stand alone before God and give an account of his life. I cannot blame others for my life, any more than Adam could blame Eve for eating the forbidden fruit. I am responsible for my choices. I have to trust God and obey him, whether or not those close to me obey him. If I have disobeyed, I have sinned. I need to repent.

Christian life begins with repentance that leads to conversion. Repentance, therefore, implies a radical individualism – a person assuming responsibility for their life. A Hindu, for example, cannot say that I have to worship my *Ishtdev*, because my family has worshipped this god for generations. In India, religion had been a tool of social control over a person's conscience, an instrument for quashing a person's individuality. In contrast, when Jesus called his disciples to 'forsake all' for the Kingdom of God, he set them free to be themselves; to follow God and fulfil their destiny – their calling. Christ's disciples, as a result, became heroes who turned the world upsidedown. Sixteenth-Century Reformers, and Nineteenth-century missionaries who followed Carey's initiative, resembled Christ's apostles at this point.

We should be grateful that some parts of the Indian Church today have recaptured Carey's missionary vision and the individual heroism that accompanies it. They seem to be the best hope for India's marginalized millions.

The above is not to imply that all facets of Western

individualism are good or rooted in the teaching of the Bible. One stream of individualism also sprang from Enlightenment thinking, summed up in the ethic of 'self-reliance' by Emerson. This increasingly dominant form of individualism turns individual self-reliance into selfishness. Carey's individualism, like his Lord's, was both self-sacrificing and balanced by the biblical emphasis on being a 'body'.

The church as a body

The Serampore trio – Carey, Marshman and Ward – generated immense power for bringing about spiritual, intellectual, and social change in India because they believed that they were called to be a 'body'. They sought to obey their call and lived as a community – sharing a common purse and a common mission.

The church is not meant to be a collection of heroes, but a community knit together by love – a fruit of the Holy Spirit. If Carey had failed at this point he would have been forgotten a long time ago. He was the leader. He stood tall above the others, but without their support his endeavours would have amounted to little. He needed them for even such basic requirements as looking after his own children, since his first wife, Dorothy, had tragically become mentally ill and required constant care herself.

Hinduism as a religion had divided people into castes. This was a primary source of India's weakness. Foreign invaders were able to come here with small armies, and conquer and rule a large populace by exploiting the inherent divisions in the Subcontinent. Carey wanted to strengthen India by uniting people across the caste barriers. He knew that through the Gospel, God himself was uniting people into one bond, a body, that is, a church.

The church was inaugurated, supernaturally, on the day of Pentecost (Acts 2). On that day the Holy Spirit had given the disciples the ability to speak the languages of all the nations from where the devout had gathered in Jerusalem for the festival. That event was the great reversal of the incident of Genesis 11, when, supernaturally, mankind was divided (as a punishment) into different language groups. The plot of the book of Acts is centred around the events through which God united the Aramaic speaking Jewish believers with those who spoke Greek; and both the groups with the Samaritans (who were the 'untouchable' half-Jews); and then, the Jewish believers with the hated 'Gentiles'. The Jews did not allow men and women to worship together; the Gospel made them one. It also united the slaves with the freed men into one body.

This understanding that through the church God was creating a new race, a body for himself, naturally forced Carey to reform the very structure of Indian society. He resolved that caste would be broken in his church; that all who become God's children by faith in Christ must become equal members of God's household.

The schools and the college at Serampore taught children of all castes in the vernacular in an attempt to break down caste. In contrast, many English-medium schools and colleges, started and run by Christians who followed Carey, catered mainly to high-caste Hindus – as a matter of policy and convenience! This had tragic consequences; Christian education was gradually swallowed up by the very evil that it was seeking to eradicate. The seats in these institutions were first filled by the high-caste students and later, the same graduates who retained caste prejudices became teachers. This fact prepared an English-speaking casteist élite to recapture the whole nation when the British were ready to pack up and leave. This élite considered themselves 'modern' because they spoke English rather than Sanskrit. But for all practical purposes, their medieval mentality has continued to this day. It weakens India by permitting an elitist language as a barrier that divides Indians from each other.

Thus the Christian English-medium education, tragically became the chief means of undermining the modernization of India; of handing India back to the slavery of Brahmanism. In the last century itself, the low-caste social reformers such as Mahatma Jotiba Phule of Pune, had seen the disastrous consequence of this compromise with the evil of caste, and the denial of the Christian truth of the equality of all men. Phule's followers, Dr Bhimrao Ambedkar for example, rightly saw that an emasculated Christianity had ceased to be of much value to the downtrodden in India. Therefore, he chose to try Buddhism, as a possible hope for the oppressed yearning to be freed from the slavery of caste.

The Gospel as the power of God for total salvation

Conservative Christians have admired William Carey because he reawakened the church to its commission to evangelize the world. Theologically liberal Christians have admired him because he triggered India's Social Reform Movement. Historians, both Christians – such as G.A. Oddie – and non-Christians such as Sen Gupta – have misunderstood Carey's social action as being incidental to his passion to 'save souls'.

The truth, however, is clear from his *Enquiry* that even before coming to India, Carey had understood that nothing would dispel the social darkness of India, save the spread of the Gospel.

Carey knew the Gospel to be the only effective antidote to social evils, besides, of course, being the divinely ordained means of the eternal salvation for our souls. This conviction sustained Carey's chief labour: to make the

Bible available to the Indian masses in their own languages.

It is worth repeating that our mistake today is that some who believe the Gospel look upon it merely as a means of private salvation (for going to heaven). They do not seem to realize that the Gospel is the God-given 'public truth'- the means of organizing a decent society. Therefore, their faith becomes privately engaging but publicly irrelevant. On the other hand, those 'Christian' activists who do not believe the basic truth of the Gospel, that Jesus Christ died and rose again for our sin, attach themselves to ideologies that are most popular in their day. For example, some of my friends, until recently, prided themselves on being Christian-Marxists or Socialists. In contrast to both the Conservatives and the Liberals, William Carey knew that Jesus is the 'Light of the world' – not just the One who lights the way to heaven. He sought to reflect that Light in the world.

Unfortunately many Christians today who are sincerely trying to serve society are oblivious of the power that God has already given to us to dispel darkness. They tend to put their hope for social change primarily in their own projects. Thus, it appears that their main anxiety is how to keep getting financial aid for their particular programmes. I know many projects which survive only because the project holders are willing to bribe officials, i.e., participate in one of the main evils of Indian society today.

Why have we sunk to this level? I suggest that this is a result of the materialistic presupposition of our age. Since the time of Karl Marx many have assumed, often unconsciously, that material reality is basic and that moral/intellectual/spiritual aspects of reality are secondary – by-products of economics. Carey, on the other hand, believed that the real battle is in the mind. False beliefs lead to wrong behaviour and harmful culture. Therefore, Carey strove to fill the Indian mind with the truth of God's word. That, he understood, was conversion – the cornerstone in the task of civilizing.

Conclusion

In *A New History of Methodism*, W.J. Townsend wrote,

> Important eras of human progress and national salvation are generally inaugurated and moulded by a man who has understanding of the times, whose ear is open and attuned to respond sympathetically to the sighs and groans of humanity for redemption from the powers of evil, and who has the constructiveness and comprehensiveness of nature to become a builder of a nation and a hero of far reaching reformation.
> These words, *adds A.H. Oussoren*, may be applied to William Carey. Just like all great leaders of humanity, he not only understood his own time, but also had a clear conception of the times before him. He saw their corruption, their baseness, their frivolity, their deplorable state of affairs everyday...

But unlike most of us, Carey never gave up hope for India because he looked beyond man, beyond society, to God's saving act in human history. Carey put his confidence for our salvation in the power of the Gospel; that is, in the power of the death and resurrection of Jesus Christ to deliver us from our sin.

Foreword To Study Guide

by *Darrow Miller*

As with most Christians, I have associated the name William Carey as the father of modern missions. Upon reading *Carey, Christ and Cultural Transformation* by Ruth and Vishal Mangalwadi, I realized that he would better be described as the father of Christian development.

As Vice-President of Staff Development for Food for the Hungry International I recognized the importance of this little book for our staff as well as for others who live and labour among the poor and hungry or seek to disciple nations.

My hope is that this study guide will enable those who use it to reflect more deeply and personally on the importance of William Carey's life for our own time.

For the Kingdom coming.

Study Guide

Chapter 1

Who was William Carey? What did he believe? What values and behaviours stemmed from those beliefs and what impact did they have on India? In contrast, what are the beliefs and values of folk Hinduism and what are their consequences in the material world?

For three student monologues of your choosing, use the following charts (Beliefs,[1] Values,[2] Behaviour,[3] Consequences[4]) to identify the beliefs, values, behaviour, and consequences of both William Carey and his host folk Hindu culture. I have illustrated what this might look like for the Science student. The objective here is to begin to see the practical relationship between beliefs and behaviour. Stretch yourself, but know your limits!

---

[1] Beliefs: World views. The fundamental principles of culture. It is these that form values and ultimately the life of individuals and cultures.
[2] Values: the attitudes and ethos of individuals and cultures.
[3] Behaviour: the day-to-day external life-styles of people. A manifestation of values.
[4] Consequences: The final results of one's behaviour; the ultimate ends of one's belief system.

Student of Science: (Example)

	William Carey	**Hinduism**
Beliefs	*Creation is created; it is good.*	*Nature is 'maya'/ illusion. 'All is one.'*
Values	*All works praise your name. Nature worthy of study. Insects are creatures worthy of our attention.*	*Nature is to be shunned. Insects are souls in bondage. Insects are as valuable as man.*
Behaviour	*Meticulously observed plants in India Brought English daisy. Intro Linnaean system to gardening. Published books on science & natural history. Lectured on science.*	Do not destroy pests who eat grain.
Consequences	Stimulated interest in science and food production	Decreased food supplies available for people

Student of _____ :

	William Carey	**Hinduism**
Beliefs		
Values		
Behaviour		
Consequences		

Student of _____ :

	William Carey	Hinduism
Beliefs		
Values		
Behaviour		
Consequences		

Student of _____ :

	William Carey	Hinduism
Beliefs		
Values		
Behaviour		
Consequences		

2. Who was William Carey? Describe in your own words!

----

3. If you had an impression of him before you read this chapter, how has that perception changed?

----

4. William Carey was principle-centred in his development work. Articulate one to three principles that were important for Carey.

----

5. What did you learn about the importance of a belief system for a people's values, behaviour and the consequences in terms of the societies they build?

----

6. Why is it important to disciple nations at the level of their practical belief system?

Chapter 2

We have been so conditioned by our culture that we tend to accept the materialist's paradigm of reality and analyze poverty from a secular perspective. William Carey saw and acted through a biblical set of glasses.

1. According to Ruth Mangalwadi, what created the physical poverty for the women of Calcutta (p. 10, 13)?

----

2. In his letter to John Williams (p. 11) Carey wrote 'But a people can hardly be better than their gods.' This parallels Psalm 115:1–8. The psalmist concludes: 'Those who make them will be like them...' (115:8). [We become like the gods that we worship.] Describe the 'Hindu mind' (p. 11-12):

----

3. What do you think is meant by 'false principles' (p. 11)?

----

4. The 'false principles' enslave individuals and whole cultures (*ethnos*). *How has sin enslaved Hindu culture (p. 12-14)? Give specific examples of how the belief system impoverished Indian women:*

----

5. Think of your own cultural context. What practice do you see that has led to the impoverishment of women?

----

6. What 'false principles' lie behind the practices?

----

7. What was Carey's strategy to free women from poverty (p. 25-26)?

----

8. What Biblical principles was Carey operating from?

----

9. How can Carey's insights and methodology be applied to facilitate development in the communities where you work?

----

10. What is the role of Scripture in setting people free from poverty? What is the foundation for true freedom (p.26–7)? Where does development begin?

----

11. Illustrate how your team is currently or could consciously use the Scriptures to lay a 'theological foundation for a belief in the sacredness of life'? How do you expect this to impact the communities where you are working?

----

12. What, if any, are the implications for you in the community where you live?

Chapter 3

We are reminded that it is through the cracks in the clay of the jar that the light emanates. Identify one or two 'cracks' in your life. How is/can God shine his light through those cracks?

----

1. Dorothy Carey's Sacrifice

– What was Dorothy Carey's sacrifice?

– If you could have give William Carey one piece of Godly counsel concerning his marriage and life's work, what would it be?

– From what you have learned from 'Dorothy Carey's Sacrifice' write a proverb or define a principle that captures the essence of this story.

----

2. A Beautiful Marriage

– What is a soulmate?

– God desires that we grow in Christ. Carey knew a marriage both with and without a soulmate. How does a marriage with a soulmate contribute to Christian maturity?

- How does a marriage without a soulmate contribute to Christian maturity?

---

3. Creative Leisure

- How did Carey work to balance his life between being active and reflective?

- How is the balance in your life? How do you use your leisure time? What area(s) are you willing to work on to become more mature in this area of your life?

---

4. Beauty Out of the Ashes

- Have you had a loss in your life like Carey's? If you have, please describe it.

- How did you respond?

- What did God teach you through the tragedy?

– What can we learn from Carey's response to the de
  struction of his 'life's work'?

----

5. Conflicts in Community

– Where did Carey face some of his greatest challenges?

– What do you think he contributed to these conflicts?

– How is Carey's response instructive to you? What
  can you learn from his response?

  – Identify a person with whom you have a conflict.
    What could you do or what attitude could you ex
    hibit that would help restore the relationship.

Chapter 4

1. What was the British attitude towards India (p. 54-6)?

----

2. How did the reformer's attitude contrast to that of the 'British' (p. 56)?

----

3. Describe Carey's understanding of the relationship between the Gospel and development (p. 62-4):

----

4. What are the implications of this for people who are living and working among the poor?

----

5. What were the three assumptions that informed Carey's work; in each case, what is the application of this for the transformation of poverty into bounty?

----

6. All peoples are storytellers. All cultures have their own stories about what is real and how the world works. If a society is to be transformed, society's story must be transformed. While William Carey was working to change the 'cultural myth' of Hinduism in India, William Wilberforce and Charles Grant were working to change the story in the British Parliament and the East India Company.

7. Changing the Story: What is/are the cultural myth(s) that contribute to moral, intellectual, spiritual, social, or physical poverty in your community or nation?

----

8. Give an illustration of how you could begin to change the story in your community.

Chapter 5

1. What is the central thesis of this chapter (p. 87)?

----

2. Why is it important to examine one's 'theological' assumptions or basic belief system?

----

3. Why is it important to examine the basic belief system of the people in a community?

----

4. Let's examine William Carey's basic belief system, its general importance for community development or discipling nations. Use the following grid to record your observations about Carey's theological assumptions:

	What was Carey's basic belief about each of the following?	What is the importance of this basic belief for community development
God as the Creator		
Human beings as God's image		
God calls individuals		
The church		
The Gospel		

Overview:

What have you learned about William Carey, 'the father of modern mission'?

How has your thinking about development been changed?

List five ways your insights from this book will help you better achieve your goals where you live.

Appendix One

Biography Of William Carey

Date Of Birth: 17 August 1761

Place Of Birth: Paulers Pury, near Northampton, England.

Grandparents: Peter and Ann Carey. Peter was a weaver who later became a teacher.

Parents: Edmund & Elizabeth Carey. Edmund was also a weaver-turned-school-master.

Education: Home-schooled by his father from age six to age fourteen. Apprenticed as a shoemaker to Clarke Nichols of Piddington, and at the same time taught himself Theology, Latin, Greek and Hebrew. His parents 'drilled' the Bible into him.

Religious Background: John Warr, a fellow apprentice in the shoemaker shop led him to Christ. Thomas Scott's preaching strengthened him in his faith.

Marriages: (1) To Dorothy Plackett on 10 June 1781. She died on 8 December 1807.

(2) To Charlotte Rumohr on 8 May 1808. She died on 30 May 1821.

(3) To Grace Hughes in 1823. She died in 1835.

Missionary Society: Baptist Missionary Society founded in England on 2 October 1792.

Influential Writing: *An Enquiry Into The Obligations Of Christians, To Use Means For The Conversion Of The Heathens.* (1792)

Travel To India: Arrived in Calcutta, 11 November 1793, and never returned to his homeland, England.

Before Serampore: Resided in Bandel, Manicktullo, Sunderban, and Malda until 10 January 1800.

Serampore: Arrived Serampore 10 January 1800, and made it his headquarters. He preferred to call his mission, the 'Serampore Mission' instead of the 'Baptist Mission'.

Translations: Translated, with the help of pundits, the entire Bible in Bengali, Oriya, Hindi, Marathi, and Sanskrit. Partial translations were made in Panjabi, Pashto, Kashmiri, Telugu, Konkani. He also translated smaller portions of the Bible in twenty-three other languages and dialects.

In Calcutta: Appointed tutor at Fort William College on 8 April 1801, and taught until 31 May 1830.

Children: Seven: (1) Ann, (2) Felix, (3) William, (4) Peter, (5)Lucy, (6) Jabez, and (7) Jonathan.

Death: 9 June 1834.

Appendix Two

A One-Act Play: 'The sabbath Carey did not keep'

CAST: William Carey, Narrator, Servant, Marshman, a man, a woman, a young widow, and a boy.

NARRATOR – Today is Sunday, December 4, 1829. Carey is preparing his Sunday sermon.

CAREY - *(Sitting, reads out Isaiah 58:6–7, from his Bengali Bible.)* Is not this the kind of fasting I have chosen: to loose the chains of injustice and untie the cords of the yoke, to set the oppressed free and break every yoke?

Is it not to share your food with the hungry and to provide the poor wanderer with shelter - when you see the naked, to clothe him, and not to turn away from your own flesh and blood?

(There is a knock at the door.)

CAREY – Come in, please.

SERVANT – *(Walks in.)* This, sir, is from Lord Bentinck.

CAREY - *(Opening the envelope.)* What could the Governor General send on a Sunday morning?

(Reads a bit silently. Then presses the paper against his chest, jumps up, and exclaims.)

How wonderful! Praise God! Victory, at last!

(Shouts to Marshman in the other room.) Brother Marshman!

MARSHMAN – *(Comes running.)* What's the matter?

CAREY – Here; Look! *Sati* is now officially banned! No sabbath for me today. Could you please preach in the worship this morning? I will translate this edict into Bengali.

MARSHMAN – Praise the Lord, and congratulations to you, brother. I will gladly substitute for you. You stay here, we will celebrate this victory with worship and thanksgiving on behalf of our Indian sisters.

CAREY – *(To the servant.)* Could you please go to the home of the Bengali pundit? Request him to come as soon as he can for some urgent translation work.

(As the servant and brother Marshman walk out, Carey remembers...)

NARRATOR – *(To the congregation.)* Imagine, we are on the island of Sagar two hundred years ago, watching a religious festival held every winter at this holy place where the river Hooghly, a branch of the Ganges, meets the Bay of Bengal.

A BARE-CHESTED MAN – *(Stands prayerfully with folded hands and then jumps into the sea as the narrator comments:)*

NARRATOR – This man is offering his life as a sacrifice to the god of the sea as the highest degree of holiness. He hopes to secure immediate salvation in this way.

A WOMAN – *(Lovingly hugs her child and throws it into the sea as the narrator claps and asks the congregation:)*

NARRATOR – Please clap. This woman gives to the goddess Ganges her firstborn, in pledge for her second child. She is sacrificing the fruit of her body for the sins of her soul.

A YOUNG WIDOW – *(Walks up and lies down on a funeral pyre. A young boy lights a fire next to her while the narrator says:)*

NARRATOR – This young widow lies on the corpse of her husband, her god. The funeral pyre is being lit by her oldest, her ten-year-old son. She is committing *sati*, to go and serve her husband-god in the other world.

CAREY – *(Pulls out the letter in which he had described his first encounter with* sati *thirty years ago, and his failed attempt to prevent it. He reads the letter aloud to himself, walking up and down the length of the room.)*

'We saw a number of people assembled on the riverside. I asked for what they were met, and they told me; to burn the body of a dead man. I enquired if his wife would die with him; they answered yes, and pointed to her. She was standing by the pile of large billets of wood, on the top of which lay her husband's dead body. Her nearest relative stood by her, and near her was a basket of sweetmeats.

'I asked if this was her choice, or if she was brought to it by any improper influence. They answered that it was perfectly voluntary. I talked till reasoning was of no use, and then began to exclaim with all my might against what they were doing, telling them it was shocking murder. They told me it was a great act of holiness, and added in a very surly manner that if I did not like to see it, I might go further off, and desired me to do so. I said that I would not go, that I was determined to stay and see the murder, against which I should certainly bear witness at the tribunal of God.

'I exhorted the widow not to throw away her life; to fear nothing, for no evil would follow her refusal to be burned. But in the most calm manner she mounted the pile, and danced on it with her hands extended, as if in the utmost tranquillity of spirit.

'Previous to this the relative, whose office it was to set fire to the pile, led her six-times round it – thrice at a time. As she went round, she scattered the sweetmeats amongst the people who ate them as a holy thing. This being ended, she lay down beside the corpse, and put one arm under its neck and the other over it, when a quantity of dry cocoa leaves and other substances were heaped over them to a considerable height and then *ghee* (melted butter) was poured on the top. Two bamboos were then put over them, and held fast down, and fire put to the pile which immediately blazed very fiercely, owing to the dry and combustible materials of which it was composed.

'No sooner was the fire kindled than all the people set up a great shout of joy invoking *Siva*. It was impossible to have heard the woman, had she groaned, or even cried aloud, on account of the shoutings of the people; and again it was impossible for her to stir or struggle, by reason of the bamboos held on her like the levers of a press. We made much objection to their use of these, insisting that it was undue force to prevent her getting up when the fire burned. But they declared it was only to keep the fire from falling down. We could not bear to see more, and left them, exclaiming boldly against the murder, and filled with horror at what we had seen.'

NARRATOR – It was appropriate that he who had lodged the first protest with the Government, and more than any other man, had striven for this inhumanity's forbiddance should be used to announce the edict banning it. Oft the Scripture burned in his heart,

'Rescue those being led away to death; hold back those staggering toward slaughter. If you say, 'but we knew nothing about this,' does not he who weighs the heart perceive it? Will he not repay each person according to what he has done?' [*Proverbs 24:11–12*]

Sources

1. James R. Beck, *Dorothy Carey*; Baker Book House; Grand Rapids, Michigan; 1992.
2. Ian Bradley, *The Call To Seriousness: The Evangelical Impact On The Victorians*; Macmillan, New York; 1976.
3. S. Pearce Carey, *William Carey*; Hodder & Stoughton, London; 1824 ed.
4. William Carey, *An Enquiry*; Baptist Missionary Society, Oxfordshire; 1991.
5. Sunil Chatterjee, *William Carey & His Associates in the Awakening of Bengal*; Rachna Prakashan, Calcutta; 1974.
6. Sunil Chatterjee, *Hannah Marshman: The First Woman Missionary In India*; S.S.Chatterjee, Hooghly; 1987.
7. M. Drewery, *William Carey: Shoemaker and Missionary*; Hodder and Stoughton, London; 1978.
8. Michael Edwards, *A History Of India*; Farrar, Straus & Cudahy, New York; 1961.
9. J.N. Farquhar, *Modern Religious Movements In India*; Macmillan Company, New York; 1951.
10. Nalin C. Ganguly, *Raja Ram Mohun Roy*; YMCA Publishing House, Calcutta; 1934.
11. Kenneth W. Jones, *The New Cambridge History Of India*; Cambridge University Press, Cambridge; 1989.
12. Dick Keyes, 'Pluralism, Relativism and Tolerance' in *The Seer*, no. 7; Nivedit Good Books Distributors Pvt. Ltd., Mussoorie, U.P. India, 248 179; 1991.
13. K. S. Latourette, *A History Of the Expansion of Christianity*. 7 Vols. Eyre and Spottiswoode, London; 1938–45.
14. Vishal Mangalwadi, *Truth and Social Reform*; Hodder & Stoughton, London; 1989.

15. Vishal Mangalwadi, *When The New Age Gets Old: Looking For A Greater Spirituality*; InterVarsity Press; Downers Grove, Ill.; 1993. (British edition is called *In Search Of Self: Beyond The New Age*; Hodder & Stoughton, London.)

16. Vishal Mangalwadi, *The Missionary Conspiracy: Letters To A Postmodern Hindu*; Nivedit Good Books Distributors Pvt. Ltd, New Delhi; 1995.

17. Shakuntala Narasimhan, *Sati*; Viking, New Delhi; 1990.

18. Stuart Piggin and John Roxborough, *The St. Andrews Seven*; The Banner Of Truth Trust, Edinburgh; 1985.

19. G.A. Oddie, *Social Protest In India*; Manohar, New Delhi; 1979.

20. Rosalind O'Hanlon, *Caste, Conflict and Ideology: Mahatma Jotirao Phule and Low Caste Protest In Nineteenth-Century Western India*; Cambridge University Press, Cambridge; 1985.

21. A.H. Oussoren, *William Carey: Especially His Missionary Principles*; A.W.Sijthoff, Leiden; 1945.

22. John Pollock, *Wilberforce*; Lion, Herts; 1977.

23. E.D. Potts, *British Baptist Missionaries in India 1793–1837: The History of Serampore and Its Mission*; Cambridge University Press, Cambridge; 1967.

24. Francis A. Schaeffer, 'A Christian Manifesto' in *The Complete works of Francis Schaeffer Vol. 5*; Solway; Carlisle, U.K; 1995 Crossway Books; Wheaton, Ill.; 1982.

25. George Smith, *The Life Of William Carey*; John Murray, London; 1887

26. George Smith, *The Life Of Alexander Duff*; Hodder & Stoughton, London; 1879

27. W. Stewart, *The Plan and the Sequel: The Missionary Purpose and Legacy of William Carey and Alexander Duff*; Council Of Serampore College, Serampore; 1980.